Smart Guide™
to
Making
Wise
Investments

About Smart Guides™

Welcome to Smart Guides. Each Smart Guide is created as a written conversation with a learned friend; a skilled and knowledgeable author guides you through the basics of the subject, selecting out the most important points and skipping over anything that's not essential. Along the way, you'll also find smart inside tips and strategies that distinguish this from other books on the topic.

Within each chapter you'll find a number of recurring features to help you find your way through the information and put it to work for you. Here are the user-friendly elements you'll encounter and what they mean:

The Keys

Each chapter opens by highlighting in overview style the most important concepts in the pages that follow.

Smart Money

Here's where you will learn opinions and recommendations from experts and professionals in the field.

Street Smarts

This feature presents smart ways in which people have dealt with related issues and shares their secrets for success.

Smart Sources

Each of these sidebars points the way to more and authoritative information on the topic, from organizations, corporations, publications, web sites, and more.

Smart Definition

Terminology and key concepts essential to your mastering the subject matter are clearly explained in this feature.

F.Y.I.

Related facts, statistics, and quick points of interest are noted here.

The Bottom Line

The conclusion to each chapter, here is where the lessons learned in each section are summarized so you can revisit the most essential information of the text.

One of the main objectives of the *Smart Guide to Making Wise Investments* is not only to provide basic investment information, but to make you smarter about money and other important financial concerns to ensure a lifetime of security for yourself and your family.

Smart Guide™

to

Making Wise Investments

Gordon K. Williamson

CADER BOOKS

John Wiley & Sons, Inc.

New York • Chichester • Weinheim • Brisbane • Singapore • Toronto

This publication is designed to provide accurate and authoritative information in regard to the subject matter covered. It is sold with the understanding that the publisher is not engaged in rendering professional services. If professional advice or other expert assistance is required, the services of a competent professional person should be sought.

ISBN 0-471-29608-2

10 9 8 7 6 5 4 3 2 1

Contents

Introduction

There are literally thousands of different places you can invest your money. The purpose of this book is to help you understand the different investment categories and how your money should be invested. Investing may seem too confusing or sophisticated, but it does not have to be that way. In a short period of time you will learn what you should and should not be doing with your money.

The world of investing is divided into three camps: equity, debt and hybrid. "Equity" means that you own part or all of the asset (e.g., a business, piece of real estate, common stock, etc.). "Debt" means that you have lent out your money to someone else in return for a specific or variable-rate of return (e.g., bank CDs, money market accounts, government securities, and all categories of bonds). "Hybrid" means that the investment has some equity as well as some debt characteristics (e.g., balanced mutual funds and variable annuities that invest in stocks and bonds, convertible securities that can be changed from bonds to stocks, and high-yield bonds that often react to news in the same way that stocks do). Every type of investment, past, present, and future, falls into one of these three categories.

Some of the chapters cover individual securities and assets such as stocks and bonds. Other chapters detail specific investment vehicles that comprise these different securities and assets. The pros and cons of buying these assets individually or as part of a packaged product (e.g., mutual funds, variable annuities, and real estate investment trusts) are provided in order to help you make a more informed decision.

Several investments and professionally managed products were intentionally left out, either because their track record is horrible or their risk-adjusted returns are poor. Such investments include: options, penny stocks, limited partnerships, futures (trading in commodities), collectibles such as rare coins and stamps, and hard assets such as gold and silver.

With close to 20 years of investment advisory experience, I can say without hesitation that if you can just avoid the bad investments, you are about 60% of the way to a successful financial future. The remaining 40% of the equation has to do with having the discipline to invest or add money whenever possible, being patient, and understanding what investments are appropriate for your particular circumstances. What is appropriate for you is simply a function of your goals, time horizon, risk level, and tax bracket.

Reading this book is just the first step. What will make you successful is the implementation of what you have read and learned. Investing can appear confusing, but it does not have to be. By following the tips and game plan laid out in this book you can become a successful investor. Not all of your investing will turn out as expected; at times parts of your portfolio will perform better or worse than expected. Do not despair. This is the nature of investing. The price you will pay for achieving your financial goals is the ups and downs of the marketplace. Once you accept this volatility, the journey will become more enjoyable.

Why Invest?

We all know, at some level, that we should invest for our future. All the same, many people find acting on that knowledge a tricky proposition. Sometimes we need motivation to take action on our own behalf. That is what this chapter is all about.

My own interviews with investors indicate that there are five big reasons people take action and begin investment plans. Whatever your reason might be is not nearly as important as the motivation to actually begin a plan and then stick to it. Let us look at each of the five major reasons, in order of priority.

Retirement

This is the number one reason why people set up investment plans. Inevitably, people realize that the most important retirement safety net is the one they themselves create. Being strapped for cash when you are past your peak earning years is not much fun.

Many years ago, Social Security was a great deal: You contributed payments, and by the time you retired you would recoup all of your contributions within a relatively short period of time. So someone like my father, who retired in the mid-1970s, got back all of his Social Security contributions via the benefits he received within a couple of years. From that point on it was gravy. So Social Security was (and remains) a great deal for him.

Times have changed. For somebody who starts paying into the system now or has been in the system for even ten to fifteen years, the deal is not anywhere near as appealing. In my case, for instance (I'm 45), the amount of money I put in will pretty much equal the amount of money I'm going to take out—assuming the fund survives any future financial challenges. Actually, though, the amount I receive is going to represent less than what I paid, because even though my benefits are going to increase, they will probably not increase enough to offset the true rate of inflation. Relying on Social Security as one's primary source of income during retirement, as most people now know, is a big mistake.

Given the likely influence of inflation and the number of years I will be paying into the system, I probably won't get back much more from Social Security than what I put in, unless I live to be a hundred.

The sad fact is that the Social Security system has more than its fair share of serious problems. For one thing, benefits have not kept pace with inflation. For another, the fund always seems to be on the verge of a financial crisis, perhaps because the government keeps tapping into it to fund other programs. Heavy media coverage of the fund's problems and of personal financial issues in general has led to greater awareness of the importance of planning for retirement.

The Six Myths About Retirement

1. Seventy-Five Is the Magic Number

Life expectancy tables show that the typical American lives for seventy-five years. This figure is misleading for several reasons. This "average" includes the 20 percent of the population who die before reaching retirement, before age sixty-five. In reality, a man who reaches age sixty-five will probably live to age eighty-five. A female will likely reach age eighty-nine, because women live longer than men do. And even these figures of eighty-five for a man and eighty-nine for a woman are projections based on current medical technology and include both smokers and nonsmokers. Life expectancy is only going to increase from this point onward. Consider that at the beginning of the twentieth century, life expectancy for the average American was fifty years of age.

2. Preserving Principal Will See You Through

Unless you have a net worth of roughly half a million dollars—excluding the equity in your home or you have a pension whose increases are tied to the true rate of inflation, preservation of principal is not enough. You need to make sure your asset base grows each year, if for no other reason than to offset the rate of inflation.

A lot of people believe that their home is going to provide them with a hedge against inflation when they need it later. The truth is that much of the rise we associate with rising real estate values is driven by demographic factors not likely to repeat themselves—namely, the emergence of the two-income household. What is more, steep and unexpected declines in real estate value are quite possible, as witnessed by most of the country in the very late 1980s up to the mid-1990s.

3. My Income Is Going to Drop, So My Tax Bill Will, Too

The true tax rate, which is also known as the effective rate, has been increasing for most people ever since Congress ratified the Sixteenth Amendment (by a single vote) in 1913. Federal income tax rates may have declined during certain periods of time, particularly during the last twenty or thirty years, but the value of exemptions have also dropped. There have been many increases in local taxes, and for many there is now taxation of Social Security benefits. For most of us, even when income drops, the same old tax bite is there, but it is hidden in various creative ways. Look at gasoline taxes, which are a lot higher now than they were five or ten years ago. State income taxes, for the most part, are higher. Property taxes can rise, whether or not your income drops. Most people are shocked to learn the actual tax burden they are bearing, and how much higher it is than their nominal federal income tax bracket.

4. Medicare Will Cover It

Young adults who believe this are in for a rude awakening. Medicare covers only about half of medical health care costs, and then only for those sixty-five or older. Do not count on lots of support from the private sector: Starting in 1993, corpora-

STREET SMARTS

Melanie, concerned about the inadequacy of Social Security as a retirement income source, looked into an individual retirement account (IRA). Even though her tax bracket and her participation in another qualified retirement plan meant Melanie was not able to deduct her contributions from her income taxes, it still made sense for Melanie and her husband Rob each to set aside $2,000 a year via a Roth IRA, which allows money to grow and compound tax-free (rather than tax-deferred). She learned that, over a thirty-year period, assuming a 12 percent rate of growth, the combined annual contributions would turn into a $5 million nest egg. An 8 percent interest rate would yield $400,000 a year in income for Rob and Melanie, and would leave several million dollars for their children.

tions were required to start accounting for health care benefits in a new way, and this increased their realization of how much they were paying for health care. As a result, they have reduced those benefits and employees now have to pay a much larger share.

5. Couples Will Be Supporting Only Themselves

In the past, most parents had finished paying for their children's education when they reached their early fifties. This generally left them another ten to fifteen years to prepare for retirement. Today, raising children has been postponed by many people—narrowing the "window of preparation" and raising the very real possibility that millions of parents will find themselves on the verge of retirement still swamped with tuition bills (during the 1980s, college costs increased at twice the rate of inflation). So in many cases, homes are not going to be paid off because the occupants are going to be using home equity loans or refinancing to help pay tuition bills. Let us not forget that many of these children will land on their parents' doorsteps after graduation—or that a large number of these parents are also children who will bear the financial burden of caring for their own longer-living parents and in-laws.

6. If You Have a Pension, You Do Not Need to Worry about a Thing

People have also seen that pension plans are not as secure as they were once thought to be. Many pensioners who thought they had a secure financial future learned to their dismay that they really did not. Why? This was either because inflation was much higher than it had been projected to be when they retired or because their former employers pared down benefits payments—with virtually no repercussions from the legal system. For over a decade, huge corporations with financial obligations to pensioners have reneged on some of their commitments to former employees, telling the courts that attempting to meet all their responsibilities would essentially bankrupt them. In virtually all cases, the courts have not penalized these firms; a lot of pensioners are seeing reduced benefits either through lower dollar amounts or exclusion of certain types of promised fringes, such as medical benefits for life.

So much for the six big myths. How should you respond to them? By taking action now to set up a realistic plan for your own retirement. When you do your retirement planning early on, you make a realistic assessment of both your current financial situation and your likely future financial requirements. You identify problems you might face during retirement (such as those discussed above) and find solutions for those future problems today. If you make a mistake and your rate of return is not as high as you thought, you have time to make up for those shortfalls. Early retirement planning also lets you set financial goals and objectives for maintaining the lifestyle you want.

Now let's return to the remaining four reasons why people invest and see what strings are attached to these reasons.

College Education

The second most popular reason people invest is to finance a college education. The projected cost of sending a child through four years of a college or university eighteen years from now is at least $250,000 for a public college or $500,000 for a private one. These estimates do not include graduate school.

Purchasing a Home

The third reason people invest is to purchase a home. This goal is generally associated with younger people who are eager to have a place they can call their own. Two-thirds of all American households own their own home; an amazingly high percentage.

The average home today nationwide costs about $175,000. If you go to a place like San Francisco, the figure is considerably higher; by the same token, if you go house-hunting in the Midwest, in some medium-size towns, you can find a fairly substantial house in the $40,000 to $80,000 range. (A friend of mine recently bought a brand-new three-bedroom, three-bath house in Arizona with a swimming pool in a nice neighborhood with a one-half acre lot for just a little over $100,000.)

More Current Income

This objective usually combines with the retirement goals. People realize that they need or would like more income; perhaps as a backup fund, in case an emergency arises. They want more money in the bank, so they invest for income and just stash cash in a checking or savings account. Or perhaps they realize that certain expenses—for example, autos, medicine, or vacations—are greater than anticipated.

By the way, contrary to what you might expect, when a couple retires, their living expenses do not drop radically. They may take a fair number of expensive trips, thinking: "Hey, we're sixty-five years old. How many more years are we going to be in good health and be able to enjoy these kinds of outings?" If a couple has some discretionary income from investments, that money pays for those trips. As they grow older, they are more likely to have medical needs, home care, and so on, and investment income may come in very handy.

Helping Those We Love

And finally, we invest to help out our loved ones. One of the most intriguing demographic trends of recent years is the return to the nest. Just when parents think they have the house to themselves, an adult child will move back home. College kids are coming back for anywhere from one to three years. And many parents end up helping out one or more of their children.

Besides these five reasons we have just examined, there are two underlying psychological ben-

F.Y.I.

You may qualify for an Education IRA. These accounts are designed to help pay for a child's postsecondary education, including tuition, fees, books, and room and board. All earnings in this type of account accumulate tax-free; an Education IRA can be used in conjunction with a standard IRA or a Roth IRA. Contributors must have an adjusted gross income (AGI) of less than $110,000 (single) or $160,000 (married). Individuals may contribute up to $500 annually on behalf of any child under age eighteen; contributions are not tax-deductible. Contributions may not continue after the child's eighteenth birthday.

efits to setting up a sensible investment plan. These may be helpful for you to know; all point toward the importance of setting up an investment plan now, rather than later.

Fewer Options as You Get Older

The older you get, the fewer options there are in the workplace. A job seeker in her late forties or in her early to mid fifties has a lot less flexibility than a younger individual. Despite the knowledge and skills older workers may bring to the workplace, the fact is that they are at a significant disadvantage in the workforce as the years go by. They often have to settle for second-tier job offers, or worse. Although age-related employment discrimination is illegal, it is nevertheless common and often extremely hard to prove. Developing a sensible investment plan now means decreasing the financial demands of your later years—and reducing your vulnerability to employment problems later on in your career.

Make It Easier on Your Family

A major concern of some investors (typically those in upper-middle-class income brackets) is to make life easier for their heirs. They want to be able to give gifts of money to their children or grandchildren or leave as large an estate as possible for them. Or perhaps they just want the security of knowing that if an emergency arises, they can tap into their portfolio without having to appeal to others and without having the problem affect their own lifestyle too dramatically.

Start Now

I mention all these points not to frighten you, but to impress upon you the importance of starting a sensible investment plan *now*—one that will help you address the many challenges you are likely to face in the years and decades ahead. To do that, and to get the most out of what follows, you need to be familiar with three basic ideas: **risk**, **diversification**, and **active versus passive management** of your investment portfolio.

Risk

As you will see a little later on in the book, even some classic conservative investments are extraordinarily risky when it comes to inflation. Any investment that does not keep pace with inflation's ability to eat away at your purchasing power is a risk, even if the people selling it identify the investment as risk-free, which they often do. True, there is virtually no chance of your losing your capital, but capital loss is only one form of risk. Eroding purchasing power, taxes, and missed opportunity costs are just some of the other types of risk.

Despite what you may hear, every investment carries some kind of risk. The question is not whether you can eliminate risk from your investments, but rather whether you can manage it intelligently, given your investment goals. The aim of a good financial plan is not to avoid high-risk investments, but to select investments that make up a balanced portfolio and are likely to bring you closer to your objectives.

Diversification

By putting your money in more than one kind of investment, you can dramatically reduce the effects of most risks associated with investing. That is because different kinds of investments do well at different times. Fortunately, what is bad for one type of investment is often good for another.

By balancing your investments wisely, you can reduce the possibility that a sudden shift in the economy or an unexpected change in market conditions for a particular group of companies will have a significant negative effect on your investments. When one category of investment declines, another may or will rise. Because you have different asset categories, your overall ride is not as bumpy as it might otherwise be if you were to concentrate on the most recent hot investment.

This balancing principle is known as diversification, and it is a hallmark of sound investing. Diversification keeps you from becoming too reliant on one portion of the market, and it protects you from inevitable economic shifts. It also protects you from your own biases and those of your investment adviser, and others.

The Active Approach versus the Passive Approach

Many people view investment strategy as a matter of picking winners—a kind of socially acceptable gambling that involves barking the words *buy* or *sell* into a telephone at thirty-second increments. Actually, there are two extremes when it comes to investing: the active approach, in which investors, professional or otherwise, constantly manipulate their holdings, and the passive approach, which involves simply buying and holding on to a particular group of investments for an extended period of time. In both schools, the question of investment selection is all-important.

Both approaches have their adherents. I suggest that individual investors be ready to develop the discipline necessary to hold on to certain kinds of investments (namely stocks, bonds and real estate) to achieve growth and take advantage of the steady growth in value of these markets. That does not necessarily mean holding on to a security or property forever, but it does mean avoiding the frenetic and expensive habit of always chasing fashionable investments and trying to guess when they will start to slide.

Making Your Money Work for You

The goal of this book is to help you get your own private "money machine" up and running, building wealth for you and your family. As you have seen, the reasons to take action right away are many and compelling.

So, what is next? Well, before you look at what is likely to work in your investment plan, let us examine what does not. Otherwise rational and knowledgeable people make some big mistakes when it comes to money matters. These mistakes are so common and so serious that they have done considerable damage to countless and otherwise sound investment plans. I have identified eight such mistakes.

1. Spending Too Quickly

Many members of the "baby boomer" generation want the same things their parents wanted—and then some. They want houses nicer than those they grew up in, and instead of the Chevy Mom and Dad drove, they may want a Lexus or a BMW. But more important, they want it now. They do not want to scrimp and save for years the way Mom and Dad did to get that first house.

Renting living space has gotten a bad rap over the years, which is too bad, because renting an affordable apartment is often a great way to save up money for a down payment on a home. As a general rule, rent prices have not even come close to keeping place with inflation over the past ten or twenty years. We may not think of renting as a bargain; after all, when a rent payment goes from $800 to $850 a month or from $600 to $650 a month, we notice it. But those increases typically do not happen every year. More to the point, such increases, percentage-wise, are often lower than the rate of inflation.

Not too terribly long ago in this country (that

is to say, when my parents were raising me), people taught their children that you did not take on debt if you could possibly avoid doing so. But today, if people want something, they just go out and finance it. That has been true for a number of years, and a good chunk of the modern economy is based on easy credit and "buy now, pay later." That kind of buying is certainly convenient, but it is also very expensive, leading people into the trap of working to pay off hefty interest fees, rather than making their money work for them. By postponing the big buys—the new house, the fancy car—these buyers will end up with nicer cars and homes because they have the "money machine" working for them.

2. Taking on Credit Card Debt

Taking on credit card debt is a major blunder, one of the biggest negatives of personal financial management. Credit cards often lead people to spend more than they really should.

Some people with quite a bit of money in investments that pay around 8 percent annually also carry huge amounts of credit card debt, for which they are paying 15 to 21 percent in interest each year. They have gotten in the habit of charging things and not paying off balances; it is a lifestyle decision that seems perfectly normal and natural to them. Periodically, credit card companies raise these people's limits. Why not? The cardholders are making their payments; they are good credit risks. If you were a credit card issuer, wouldn't you want to lend as much money as possible at 15 to 21 percent?

Do not take on credit card debt unless an

emergency arises. If you owe a large amount of money on your credit card, make repaying the total amount due a priority. And don't borrow money on the card if you can possibly avoid doing so. Finally, if you have an investment portfolio (and you will, by the time you get finished putting the advice in this book to work), get rid of your credit cards altogether if you cannot discipline yourself to pay off the outstanding balances each month. No matter how well your portfolio is doing, credit card debt can wipe out the gains.

3. Not Buying Smart

Saving a little money on lots of little things can make a big difference in your financial picture. It may not be fashionable to say so, but I'm a big fan of taking advantage of bargains. If Coca-Cola usually costs $5 a case and is on sale for $3 a case, stock up. Why? Because there are not very many investments on earth that can beat a 40 percent savings. I take the same approach to buying things like soap or toothpaste or toilet paper—anything with a long shelf life. When retailers or manufacturers offer dramatic one-time discounts, I pay attention. If I can save 20 percent or more on one or more items, I figure this is money in the bank and pick up three or four cases or containers. Few people make the connection of saving, say, 20 to 40 percent with the amount of risk necessary to even attempt to make a 20 percent annual return on an investment.

I know this kind of shopping ends up being, over the course of a year, a savings of perhaps only a hundred dollars. So why bother? Well, if you invested that $100 in a mutual fund that mirrored the S&P 500 over the next twenty years, you would end up with over $86,000. It really is a mistake not to take advantage of obvious sales.

4. Investing Too Conservatively

This is typically a problem for people in their late fifties or older. Many of these investors invest too conservatively, due to comfort level. People like investing in instruments that seem very safe. But the truth is that however much we may enjoy the idea of a guarantee, most of the things we fear in life do not ever come to pass. Basing one's entire investment strategy on avoiding virtually all risk except that of losing ground to inflation is a common and costly mistake.

Consider, for instance, that billions of dollars are in bank certificates of deposit (CDs) and other cash equivalents such as U.S. Treasury bills (T-bills)—primarily, I believe, because of the comfort level they offer investors. But the fact is that if you look over the past twenty years, CDs have lost money most years, once you adjust for inflation and income taxes. This kind of performance sounds underwhelming to me.

The fact is that even for a recently retired couple, the greatest threat to their financial stability will not be the ups and downs of the stock market, but the cumulative effects of inflation. As risky as the stock market may sound, the fact is, historically, the market goes up three out of every four years. If the fluctuations of the stock market worry you, consider using hybrid mutual funds such as balanced funds, which invest in both stocks and

STREET SMARTS

Credit card interest typically runs in the 15 to 21 percent range annually, which is too high for any investment to overcome on a regular basis. Anyone who tells you that you can earn a consistent, guaranteed rate of return of 15 to 20 percent is living in a dream world or peddling "investments" that are likely to get you into legal trouble. Most experts agree that over the long haul you can expect to earn something on the order of 12 to 14 percent annually in the stock market, over a period of ten to twenty years. If you stayed in the market for that long, began by investing the same amount you owed on an outstanding credit card bill, and paid only the minimum on that bill each month, your credit card payments would easily wipe out any gains you enjoyed in the market.

bonds, or high-yield bonds, which act somewhat like a stock and somewhat like a bond. Such instruments are much safer than people think.

There are huge amounts of money tied up in overly conservative investment instruments—typically, the kind known as classic debt instruments (bonds and money market instruments). Debt instruments, which are discussed more later in chapter 2, have historically been a bad hedge against inflation. Relying on them because of a desire to minimize risk can be a very big investment mistake, particularly over long periods of time.

5. Overreacting to Market Fluctuations

This mistake has to do with overreacting to the upside of the sales tools many companies use to sell investments and failing to acknowledge the downside in any meaningful way. Brokers, advisers, banks, and financial planners sell products, and they have sales materials meant to help them sell those products. During a meeting with a prospective customer, they will pull out what are called "mountain" charts reflecting the performance of various equity investments.

A mountain or line chart is basically a graph showing the growth of a hypothetical $10,000 investment over the last one to twenty years. People see the ups and downs in this chart, but they focus most intently on the end point, which is generally situated in the upper right-hand corner of the chart, and think, "Oh gee, how terrific that is. I'm going to get the same results in the next ten years." Well, the truth is, they probably won't.

And you know what? People selling these financial instruments know there is a problem, but they do not come out and say it. Why should they? They might lose a sale. They want that sale, and they want that commission. Moreover, a chart, table or graph does not reflect the uncertainty, fear, and frustration that investors actually go through during those rough periods.

The reality is that very few people will end up staying with that hypothetical investment. After the first sharp downturn, they will want out. Many investments require real discipline, the ability to ride out the storms represented by the up-and-down movements on that line chart. It is easy to say you plan on sticking with an investment but harder to do so when your money is taking a beating.

When you see those mountain charts, remember that they do not reflect the pain and suffering people go through when the stock market drops two hundred points in one day.

There is *always* something unsettling on the horizon. And real trouble can result when inexperienced investors decide to second-guess the stock, bond, or real estate market. Once you pull out, the tendency is to wait for certain events to happen before you start investing again. Before you go into equity investments, whether it is ownership of real estate or stocks, you need to understand that ups and downs are part of the process and resolve to live with them.

Historically, although the stock market has always been volatile, over time it has proven to be a great investment for well over a hundred years. The stock market is the only investment with that kind of history. No matter when you were born, one year ago or sixty years ago, the stock market is higher now than it was when you were born. You

SMART SOURCES

For more information on some sound strategies for overcoming market turbulence, visit the National Association of Investors web site (www.better-investing.org) and learn how its simple principles have helped investors deliver solid returns, even in times of economic uncertainty. The NAIC states that its methods have been producing financial success for individuals and investment clubs for over forty-five years.

can't say that about real estate, oil, gold, or virtually any other investment.

That is the plus side. The stock market as a whole moves upward over time. At the same time, there are all sorts of risks in investing in the stock market. There is always a crisis looming somewhere. There is always a reason not to invest this week or year. You have to understand what those crises, those little blips in the line heading toward the upper right-hand corner, are likely to look like, and you have to accept them if your investment experience is be successful.

6. Buying a New Car Every Couple of Years

There is certainly nothing wrong with a new vehicle, except that the value of it always drops significantly in the first two years. Let's say you buy a $30,000 vehicle; it will depreciate at least 20 percent in the first year. That means you absorb a $6,000 loss in the first year through depreciation alone.

Think about what that $6,000 means. That's over $15 per day, after you have paid for the car. Ask yourself: Is the privilege of owning a new car worth $15 per day, each and every day of the year? Think how much better off you would be buying a car that is one year or two years old. Let somebody else take the hit on the depreciation. You are better off spending the money on something that is going to add value, rather than lose it, like hardwood floors for your home, for example, which will last for decades and make your home more valuable.

That is really the essence of sound investing: using money in ways that will add significant value to your own financial picture. By avoiding the errors listed here, you will have gone a long way toward turning that worthy goal into a reality. Of course, it is not enough simply to avoid common mistakes: You have to have an investment plan that makes sense for you.

7. Failing to Do Any Comparison Shopping

If you were to buy a car, the odds are that you would not walk down the street and say, "I hope there is a dealership of some kind around here; I need to buy a car today." Yet people typically spend a lot more time shopping for a car or trying to get a good airline fare than they devote to investing their money. My experience is that this holds true for people investing anywhere from a few hundred dollars to several hundred thousand dollars. As a whole, people do not do the research that they would for other decisions that have far less long-term impact on their lives.

The biggest mistake is going to a seminar hosted by some "investment professional" (that is, a salesperson whose aim is to make money by handling your investments) and automatically deciding to cast your lot with that person. Before you invest, you need to interview several candidates, whether they are investment advisers, financial planners, brokers, counselors, or whatever. Such people have differing levels of expertise and are likely to deliver different kinds of value for what you pay them. Some will go out of their way to educate you. Others will not always act in your best interests, because they will not bother to

F.Y.I.

Past performance of an individual stock or equity investment has literally no bearing whatsoever on that investment's future performance. You cannot use last year's performance as a guide to predict what this or next year's performance will be for any investment. In fact, there is less than a 3 percent correlation between the performance of a stock from one year to the next and less than a 10 percent correlation for long-term U.S. Government bonds.

determine what those best interests are; they will simply pursue the same strategies they always have. If your values and needs match theirs, then there is no problem. But if there is a mismatch, you are the one who suffers.

You want to be with somebody who has the same kind of investment approach that you do, whether it is moderate, conservative, or aggressive: somebody you trust; and somebody who has experience. If you are dealing with a broker who gives you the same advice that you get from reading *Money* magazine, then odds are you are wasting your time paying any kinds of fees. You are paying something for nothing. You are better off with no-load (no commission) funds or investing on your own.

If you decide to use an adviser, shop around for someone who has at least five to ten years' experience, who devotes the necessary time, who is on the same investment wavelength as you, and who specializes in the areas that interest you, whatever those areas might be. Find out exactly what this person is going to do for you before you agree to pay for his or her services.

8. Keeping Too Much in Cash

The conventional wisdom of most experts is that you should always keep six months' worth of expense money in cash equivalents. The reality is that you want to make your money work for you. You do not need six months of cash reserves. Most of the investments you are going to make can be liquidated at any time, with little or no penalty. Moreover, there are usually alternatives if such an emergency arises.

First off, if you are employed and married and you have a working spouse, you will still have some income stream even if one of you is laid off or becomes disabled. Second, when something goes wrong, a well-structured portfolio will allow you to tap into certain parts at little or no cost. Third, keeping your assets in cash or cash equivalents means you are not earning as much as you could be because you are waiting for an emergency that probably will not arise. Making the money work for you is better than keeping it idly in cash equivalents, where you are losing ground on an after-tax and/or after-inflation basis.

The Next Step

The following chapters cover stocks, bonds, and real estate. These, along with cash and hard assets, are considered the major asset categories. Cash equivalents—for example, money market accounts, bank CDs, and interest-bearing checking accounts—are not covered because I do not consider any of them an investment.

The chapters on mutual funds and annuities introduce two different ways in which you can pool your investment money with that of countless others, and take advantage of professional management at very low cost. These chapters also explore a few strategies for limiting taxes and providing steady income as you approach retirement.

The final chapter of the book takes us full circle. It provides a financial road map, but unlike this introductory chapter, it includes specific recommendations for different risk levels, encompassing the asset categories detailed in earlier chapters.

THE BOTTOM LINE

It is doubtful that Social Security benefits will be anywhere near sufficient to provide for you by the time you retire. Particularly as corporate pension programs are curtailed and life expectancy continues to increase, people need to take control of planning and saving for retirement.

To maximize your savings, regardless of the goal, you need to start investing now. The power of investing comes from long-term growth. Properly invested, your money can double every five to eight years; fitting in more doubling periods can produce dramatic increases in your nest egg.

Remember that there's a strong link between investing and saving. The more you can postpone major purchases and keep your lifestyle in check, the more money you have to invest, and the greater the rewards further down the line.

....

The Basics of Bonds

A bond is an interest-bearing security with a maturity date—or, more simply, it's a loan. The borrower (or issuer) of a bond, be it a corporation, a federal government, or state and local governments, makes certain promises to the buyer, which usually include the payment of interest twice a year and the repayment of the loan, known as its "face value" or "redemption value." Bonds are issued with a face value of $1,000 but are usually traded in increments of five ($5,000, $10,000, $15,000, etc.). In general terms, bonds allow their issuers to borrow larger sums of money on more favorable terms than from traditional short-term lenders such as banks.

What Bonds Are

Like stocks, bonds are a negotiable financial instrument or "security." They are traded actively every day, and the value of a bond fluctuates regularly. Though all bonds are issued with a maturity date, you do not need to hold a bond until then: A bond can be bought and sold at any time, from the day it is purchased up to just before it matures.

There are a few key elements in evaluating the value and soundness of a bond:

1. The issuer

2. Credit quality

3. Interest payment

4. Maturity

Other variables can also affect a bond's value, such as general interest rates, inflation, economic conditions, and the investing public's perception of other investment vehicles. Since these are beyond the control of the issuer, we'll look at them more closely later.

The Issuer

The U.S. Government is the safest of all issuers since it has taxing power plus the ability to print more money if necessary. It also has a perfect track record: The federal government has never defaulted on the payment of interest or principal on any of its obligations.

The next most secure issuers are foreign governments of economically mature countries such as Japan, the U.K., Germany, France, Italy, and Canada (these six countries, along with the United States, are known as the "G-7 nations").

As a whole, municipalities (state and local governments) are also considered quite safe since they often have the power to tax, collect fees, and raise money from sales taxes. Some municipalities have defaulted on interest and/or principal payments, however.

Corporate issuers run the gamut from very safe to speculative. Blue-chip companies, such as IBM, GM, GE, Microsoft, and McDonald's, typically have a perfect track record and are considered to be quite safe. But young, growing, and/or troubled companies often look to the bond market for financing as well, by issuing high-yield or junk bonds, and these carry a greater measure of risk.

Credit Quality

Creditworthiness is a measure of the likelihood that a bond issuer will make good on its promises to pay interest regularly and repay the face value at maturity. Several rating services review and analyze a wide range of financial data and assign a letter grade to each issuer's bond. The exception is U.S. Government obligations, which are not rated because they are considered the ultimate in creditworthiness.

The best-known rating services are Standard and Poor's (S&P), Moody's, Fitch, and Duff and Phelps (D&P), of which S&P and Moody's are the most popular. The ratings services look closely at the issuer's track record, amount of collateral (e.g., plant and equipment), current cash flow and sales, amount of outstanding debt and its maturity, as well as projected sales and profit.

Interest Payment

Simply put, the lower a bond is rated, the greater the interest, or yield, it will have to pay in order to attract investors. The biggest jump in yield takes place when a bond drops from barely investment grade, BBB or Baa

Maturity

With very few exceptions, the longer a bond's maturity, the greater the interest rate. This is because the interest-rate risk increases over time. When interest rates go up, bond prices fall, and vice versa. And the longer the maturity of the bond, the more a rise in interest rates will cause the bond's value to drop. This is because the short-term bond-holder has less time to wait until the bond matures and the face value can be reinvested in higher-yielding bonds.

More about Interest-Rate Risk

As an example, suppose you bought a new 30-year U.S. Government bond with a six percent yield for a face value of $1,000. Every year, for the next thirty years, you would receive $60 (actually $30 every six months), and at the end of thirty years, the government would pay you back your $1,000.

But two years later, interest rates increase and the government issues new 30-year bonds at a 6.5 percent yield. The new bond will pay $65 a year for the next thirty years. To make the 6 percent bond just as attractive as the 6.5 percent bond, the market value of the 6 percent bond has to decrease. If the market price of the 6 percent bond drops from $1,000 to $940, the yield would increase from 6 percent to 6.38 percent (60 divided by 940 = 6.38 percent). Obviously, the effective yield is still lower than that of the new

Adding Up Zeros

There is another kind of bond that pays no interest at all. Known as "zero coupon bonds," these debt instruments build up interest over time, or "accrete" it, but do not pay out that interest until the bond matures. Zero coupon bonds are always purchased at a discount. If the bond is held to maturity, the difference between the purchase price and the face value is interest. Any accreted interest could be easily overshadowed by moderate or large gains or losses in market value (which would be caused by interest rates falling or rising—also known as "interest-rate risk"). Zero coupon bonds are best suited for sheltered accounts (e.g., retirement plans and variable annuities) since the interest is taxable. The exception to this is if you're purchasing municipal zeroes, which are exempt from federal income taxes and may also be exempt from state income taxes.

Bond Ratings

S&P	Moody's	Fitch	D&P	What It Means
AAA	Aaa	AAA	AAA	Extremely strong capacity to pay interest and principal
AA	Aa	AA	AA	Just slightly lower than the margins of protection offered by AAA-rated bonds
A	A	A	A	Favorable attributes but some minor risk under adverse conditions
BBB	Baa	BBB	BBB	Medium grade with adequate capacity to repay interest and principal
BB	Ba	BB	BB	Moderate protection in an unstable economy
B	B	B	B	Speculative and lacking desirable characteristics of investment-grade bonds; small assurance that principal and interest will be paid on time
CCC	Caa	CCC	CCC	In default or in danger of default
CC	Ca	CC		Highly speculative and in default or other shortcomings
C	C	C		Paying no interest; extremely poor investment quality
D	D	DD		In default of interest or principal in arrears

The top four grades (AAA, AA, A, and BBB in the case of S&P) are referred to as "investment grade" or "bank quality." Everything else is referred to as "high-yield" or "junk." Certain fiduciaries such as trusts, institutions, and retirement plans are forbidden from investing in anything but investment-grade bonds.

There are two important things to keep in mind about bond ratings. First, the descriptions that accompany the letter grades sound more negative than they really are, since default rates are historically quite low. The default of interest or principal occurs with less than 2 percent of all bonds issued. During 1996 and 1997 the rate was in the 1 percent range. The default rate for bonds that are rated B or higher is a very small fraction of 1 percent. Even when a company goes into bankruptcy, studies indicate that bondholders end up getting back somewhere between 75 and 85 percent of their money. Second, bond ratings are not infallible. There has been more than one occasion during the 1990s when a highly rated bond issuer (e.g., Korea, Kmart, and Boston Chicken) went into default or came close to it.

Here are some rules of thumb for differently rated bonds:

• The yield difference between **AAA-rated bonds** and U.S. Government securities is usually so small that one should stick with governments, which are more marketable and provide interest that is exempt from state and local income taxes. Also, the rating of a AAA-rated company can only do one of two things: remain the same or drop. A lesser-rated bond always has the possibility of getting a rating's boost.

• Bonds that are "**barely junk,**" meaning those rated BB and B, provide the best risk-adjusted returns as a general rule. Some of these bonds are "fallen angels," good companies whose ratings used to be investment grade and have a good chance of being bank quality again.

• **Lower-rated bonds**, meaning those rated BB, B, CCC or CC, have less interest-rate risk (a concept described earlier in the chapter) but greater financial risk. During good or even fair economic periods, such bonds can offer tremendous value, providing some of the highest possible yields.

Regardless of which type of bond you select, make sure it is rated similarly by at least two of the rating services, since each service has its own criteria and may even look at the same financial figures somewhat differently. And bear in mind that a bond's rating may change. If you buy individual bonds, check periodically with your broker to find out if the rating has changed.

bond, but whoever buys the bond for $940 gets a $60 bonus if the bond is held until maturity, at which point the buyer is paid $1,000. This added "bonus" is probably more than enough to make the 6 percent bond more attractive (at $940) than the 6.5 percent bond (at $1,000).

This example is quite commonplace. General interest rates often change throughout the year by at least ¼ percent or ½ percent, and often by more. The 6 percent bond described in the above example could jump back up in value from $940 to $1,000 or more if rates fell by ½ percent or more. But regardless of how much the bond increases or sinks in value, it is still worth exactly $1,000 at maturity.

What Else Affects a Bond?

Most of the time, the value of a bond is based on conditions beyond the control of the issuer. Changes in interest rates can have a tremendous impact, and these rates are driven by a variety of economic circumstances. Inflation is perhaps the greatest enemy of a bond. A rise in inflation generally leads to higher interest rates. If purchasing power decreases, then so does the value of a bond's fixed-income stream and thus the value of the bond itself. Upward or downward trends in sales, the cost of labor, the number of hours labor works each week (more hours is inflationary and vice versa), as well as the gross national product (GNP) and the value of the U.S. dollar all have an effect on inflation.

Conversely, indicators that inflation is stabilized or that prices are dropping (deflation) are good for bonds. A drop in housing starts, for example, is considered bullish for the bond market, since lessened demand means less pressure on prices and labor in all of the services and industries whose products are related to housing (e.g., timber, cement, copper, major appliances, etc.).

All of these concerns can change drastically from one day to the next or from one quarter to the next. This is why bonds can go up in value one day and down the next. A single report, news story, or announcement can change the price of a bond. This is why predicting the short-term direction of interest rates is just as difficult as trying to guess what the stock market will do.

Buying and Selling

When you buy a bond, the purchase price will either be "at par," "a discount," or "a premium"; these are terms that are common among bond traders and brokers.

• **Par** means that you purchased the bond for face value ($1,000 per bond).

• A **discount** means that you paid less than $1,000 per bond.

• A **premium** means that you spent more than $1,000 per bond.

Following the Market

The vast majority of bonds are not quoted in the newspaper because there are several thousand outstanding issues and most bonds are not "listed" —that is, they are not actively quoted by an exchange throughout the trading day. A sampling of government, corporate, and municipal bonds are given each day. *Barron's* provides a much more extensive bond listing each week. There are also bond indices that are quoted throughout the day in the financial news. The most widely watched index is called the "bellwether 30-year bond," which is simply the quoted price of a 30-year U.S. Government bond. Here is an example of a typical bond quotation from the newspaper:

Bond	Cur. Yld.	Vol.	Close	Net Ch.
IBM 8s10	7.8	300	102	+1/2

This quote is for an 8.0 percent IBM bond that matures in the year 2010 (thus, 8s of 10). The current yield is 7.8 percent, based on a closing price of $1,020 (shown as 102). For the day, this particular bond was up $5 per bond (Net Ch.: +½).

Quotations for municipal bonds are presented in the same manner as those for corporate bonds, but government bond and government agency issues are quoted differently (see below). One reason for this difference is that government securities are traded in 32nds of a point ($\frac{1}{32}$, $\frac{2}{32}$, etc.), which can at first be confusing since decimals are used (e.g., .16 = ½ point, not $\frac{16}{100}$).

Rate	Maturity	Bid	Ask	Chg.	Yld.
6	Sep 12b	102.14	102.16	-4	5.85

This quote is for a 6 percent U.S. Treasury bond (see the "b" next to Sep 12) that matures in September of the year 2012. The last bid to buy the stock was for $1,024.37 (102 plus ¹⁴⁄₃₂ of $10). The last ask price (selling price) was $1,025.00 (102 ½, or $1,020 plus ¹⁶⁄₃₂ of $10).

How Bonds Are Priced and Quoted

When bonds are traded, they are priced in "points." Each point represents $10; a bond that sells for par is worth 100 (points). If you hear that the bond market has had a bad day and is down a full point, this means that the typical bond has dropped in value by $10; the very next day, though, there may be a bond rally and bonds could be up a half point ($5) on average. Corporate and municipal bonds are usually priced in 16ths, and government securities are priced in 32nds.

If you see that a bond is priced at 101, then it is worth $1,010 (101 points times $10 per point). A bond that is selling for 97 is priced at $970 (97 points times $10 per point). Where it gets a little tricky is with the fractions. A corporate bond trading at "100 ⅝," for example, is worth $1,000 plus $6.25 (⅝ of $10), or $1,006.25. A government bond that just traded for "99 ¹⁶⁄₃₂" sold for $990 plus $5 (¹⁶⁄₃₂ of $10), or $995.

SMART SOURCES

Moody's *Bond Record* and Standard & Poor's *Bond Guide*, both published monthly, will tell you if a particular bond can be called and, if so, when and at what price. These publications also contain information on a bond's interest payment dates, maturity dates (day, month, and year), rating, coupon rate, price range, and issue price and date.

Yields

There are three types of yield: current, yield-to-maturity, and yield-to-call.

• **Current yield** is easy to calculate: Take the bond's coupon rate (which is the interest rate the issuer is paying) and divide it by the purchase price. If you buy a 7 percent bond for $1,000, then the current yield is 7 percent ($70 divided by $1,000). If, instead, you buy a 7 percent bond at a discount—for, say, $950—your current yield is 7.37 percent ($70 divided by $950). Current yield remains the same throughout your ownership of the bond.

• **Yield-to-maturity** prorates the discount or premium over the life of the bond. As an example, if you bought a $1,000 bond for $940 and the bond matures in twelve years, the extra $60 you will receive at maturity is prorated over the twelve years ($60 prorated over twelve years = $5 per year). This prorated amount is then added to the bond's current yield. If a premium is paid for the bond, then the prorated premium (the difference between the premium price and the $1,000 value at maturity) is subtracted from the current yield. Yield-to-maturity is how similar bonds are compared to one another; it is considered one of the more accurate ways to measure true return.

• **Yield-to-call** is very similar to "yield-to-maturity," but it assumes that the bond will be called away by the issuer at its call date. Most municipal bonds and many corporate bonds have a "call date," which allows the issuer to force you to redeem the bond prior to its maturity at a specified price, usually slightly over par. If your bond is "called away," you have no choice but to redeem it. The majority of bonds that have a call feature also have "call protection," meaning that the bond cannot be called away for at least the first ten years. As you might gather, "yield-to-call" is an abbreviated form of "yield-to-maturity" and therefore emphasizes a discount or premium in the purchase price.

Total Return

Total return is the most important measure of the value of a bond holding and is used to compare a bond with other investments. This figure comprises the current yield plus or minus any change in the principal. For example, if a bond has a 6 percent current yield and its price appreciates 9 percent during the year, the total return is 15 percent. On the other hand, if the same bond drops 7 percent in value for the year, its total return is -1 percent (6 to 7 percent).

All Types of Bonds

Now that you understand more about how the bond market works in general, let's look at the particular aspects of each different category of bond.

U.S. Government Securities

The marketable debt of the U.S. Government comes in one of three forms: Treasury bills, Treasury notes, and Treasury bonds. These securities are considered a "direct obligation," meaning that they are backed by the full faith and credit of our government.

• **Treasury bills** mature within three, six, or twelve months. They are issued in $5,000 increments, with a $10,000 minimum. T-bills do not pay interest but instead accrete interest and are sometimes called the original zero coupon bonds (see pages 29 and 47 for more details on how zeroes work). The difference between the purchase price and the redemption value is considered interest. T-bills never incur capital gains and rarely, if ever, are sold for less than the purchase price (and that could only occur if the bill were sold within a few days or a week or two after its purchase). T-bills are designed for individuals and institutions wanting to protect themselves from interest-rate risk.

• **Treasury notes** mature within one to ten years. They are issued in increments as low as $1,000. Notes and bonds with issued maturity or remaining maturity of five years or less are suited for investors who want a higher yield than that offered by T-bills and are willing to accept a modest amount of interest-rate risk in order to get it.

• **Treasury bonds** mature within anywhere from ten to thirty years. These typically appeal to investors who want the highest possible yield from a direct obligation of the U.S. Government and therefore are willing to accept a greater degree of risk as interest rates change.

Because of the tremendous safety offered, the U.S. Government and its agencies can borrow money at the lowest possible rates. Even so, U.S.

Government securities remain the most popular debt instruments in the world. No other country, municipality, or corporation is as secure. The strength of our government bonds lies in their track record (which is flawless), the size and diversity of our economy, and the United States' cultural, political, and military strength throughout the world.

Another benefit of owning U.S. Government securities is that their interest is exempt from state and local income taxes. So when you compare the yield of a T-bond to that of a AAA-rated corporate or foreign bond, don't forget to calculate the after-tax returns.

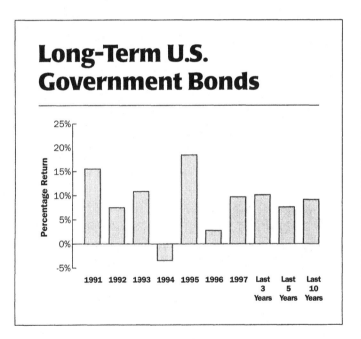

Long-Term U.S. Government Bonds

Other Federal Government Issues

Government agencies and quasi-government agencies such as FNMA (the Federal National Mortgage Association), GNMA (the Government National Mortgage Association), and FHLMC (the Federal Home Loan Mortgage Corporation) also issue bonds, but these are considered an "indirect" obligation of the government, similar to the Federal Deposit Insurance Corporation (FDIC) or the Federal Savings and Loan Insurance Corporation (FSLIC), which insure bank and savings and loan accounts for up to $100,000 per account.

Federal agency issues are considered so safe that they, like direct obligations, are not rated. For practical purposes, you can consider agency issues to be just as safe and secure as those directly issued by the U.S. Government.

These agencies all provide mortgage lenders, such as banks and savings and loan associations, with funds to lend to borrowers who are financing homes. They are all referred to as "pass-through securities," because they pay monthly income that comprises both principal and interest, just as people's monthly mortgage payments comprise a combination of principal and interest.

Lenders sell high-quality mortgages in large packages to GNMA, which resells them to the public in $25,000 increments. The lender continues to receive a servicing fee each month for continuing to service the loan and keeps any up-front fees, commissions, or points. Additionally, the lender does not have to send the mortgage money collected for GNMA for up to sixty days, thereby allowing it to be invested short-term. Lenders also receive back the face value of the mortgages immediately and have fresh money to lend out again, thereby being able to finance more homes, collect more fees and commissions, and receive more ongoing servicing fees.

Though it looks like the lenders are getting the better deal, the government does this to make mortgage money more readily available to lower- and middle-class Americans. With lower down payment requirements and somewhat lower interest rates, these types of loans enable more people to buy homes. Of course, more homeowners means more home construction, which is good for the economy overall. And a stronger economy provides more tax revenue for the government.

Investors like GNMAs because they provide monthly checks, the timely payment of which is guaranteed by a federal agency. During the early years of a GNMA, just like during the early years of a mortgage, almost the entire check represents interest. Then, as the pool of mortgages approaches maturity, more and more of each check represents a return of principal. Each check includes a notation indicating how much of it is principal, or a return of capital, and therefore not taxable, and how much represents interest, which is fully taxable.

FNMA, also known as Fannie Mae, and Freddie Mac bonds work the same way. The only difference is that these agencies do not have quite the same backing as GNMA (GNMA is a government-owned corporation, while FNMA is a publicly owned corporation sponsored by the government) and therefore pay an ever-so-slightly higher rate of return; the difference is roughly one–eighth of 1 percent more.

There are a couple of disadvantages to pass-through securities of which you should be made aware:

• Since payments in the early years represent mostly interest, many investors spend the entire amount of each check and may not replenish their principal.

• When interest rates fall and people refinance their homes, mortgages in the pool are paid off (pass-through security investors receive back their pro rata share of the mortgage repayment) and the pool becomes smaller (fewer remaining mortgages). The amount of monthly income drops, and the investor is left with some returns of principal that must now be invested at lower rates.

• Unlike direct obligations, these bonds are not tax exempt. This is the biggest reason such agency issues pay a slightly higher yield than comparable Treasury notes and bonds.

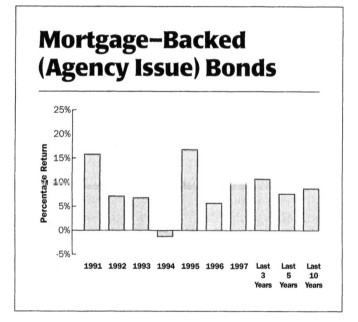

Mortgage–Backed (Agency Issue) Bonds

Municipal Bonds

Also known as tax-free bonds, municipal bonds offer interest that is exempt from federal income taxes as well as from state income taxes if the municipal bonds are issued in the same state as the investor's residence. (There are a couple of exotic exceptions, like "private purpose" bonds. To be safe, always ask your broker about any special tax conditions that may apply to a municipal bond before you purchase it.) Thus, if you live in California and buy a Los Angeles Water District bond, the interest is "double tax-exempt." But if you move to Colorado, you will owe state income tax on any interest from that California bond.

One way in which municipal bonds are classified is by their backing or collateral:

• **General obligation** (GO) bonds are those that are backed by the full faith and credit of the issuing state or government entity. Even though the power to tax is mighty, GO bonds are not all equally rated: A small town in Kansas, for example, does not have the same population or economic base as a large city in New York.

• **Revenue** bonds are backed by revenues from the project that the bonds have been issued to finance. These are issued for such things as toll roads and bridges, hospitals, sewers, and stadiums.

In general, GO bonds are considered to be slightly safer than revenue bonds. Municipal bonds overall are second in safety only to U.S. Government and federal agency issues. Municipal bonds have approximately one-third to one-half the interest-rate risk of federal and corporate

SMART SOURCES

Moody's *Bond Survey* and Standard & Poor's *Credit Week,* both published weekly, provide extensive coverage of corporate and municipal bonds. They're expensive, but are carried by many libraries.

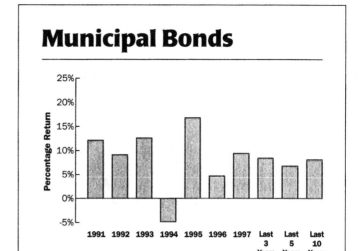

Municipal Bonds

bonds of similar quality and maturity (which means they also have less upside appreciation potential if rates drop). This is because they are one of the few remaining tax shelters and supply is limited.

Corporate Bonds

While corporate bonds have most of the same characteristics as government and municipal bonds, the major differences lie in how the bond is collateralized and whether or not it is convertible. The great majority of all corporate bonds issued are debentures, which means that the bond is backed by the general creditworthiness of the corporation, rather than by any specifically pledged assets. If a bond's collateral has been pledged by the company's financial assets, such as stocks and other bonds, then it is referred to as a "collateral trust bond." Corporate bond investors should primarily rely on the bond's rating, which takes into account all of the issues described above. The same is true when considering convertible and zero coupon corporate bonds.

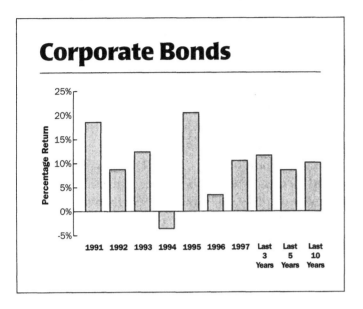

Convertibles

In order to attract a wider investor or borrower base, some corporations issue convertible preferred stock and/or convertible bonds. These securities can be converted into common stock, based on a conversion formula (i.e., each convertible bond can be exchanged for ten shares of common stock). The conversion may also contain certain restrictions (i.e., the conversion can only take place after the year 2002).

Whether or not you want to convert generally depends upon the price of the stock at any given

SMART SOURCES

You can learn more about convertible securities by subscribing to Value Line's Convertible Service (800-833-0046), or by consulting Moody's *Bond Record*.

time. As an example, if a $1,000 convertible bond can be exchanged for twelve shares of a stock that currently trades at $100 a share, the convertible bond is worth at least $1,200. And it's probably worth a little more, since the interest payment on the bond is probably greater than the dividend yield, if there is one, on the twelve shares of common stock. Of course, this value changes as the price of the stock fluctuates. You can also factor in your assessment of what the stock might do in the future.

Convertible bonds are considered a "hybrid" investment in that they possess some qualities of a bond and some qualities of a stock. Hybrids can be safer than bonds or stocks. If a convertible bond drops in value because interest rates have risen and all bonds now are worth less, that loss can be mitigated if the price of the common stock has risen. Similarly, if the stock falls, making con-

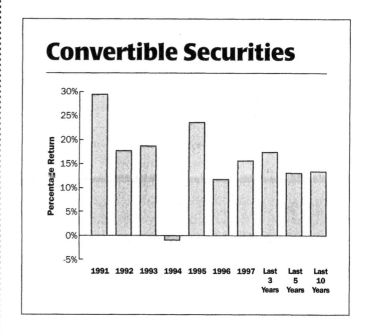

Convertible Securities

version less attractive, the value of the convertible security may still be maintained if interest rates have also fallen (causing bond prices to increase).

Zero Coupon Bonds Revisited

You can buy zero coupon municipal, corporate, and government bonds. Like other bonds, zeros come in a wide range of maturities, interest rates, and ratings. An advantage of all zero coupon bonds is that they carry no "reinvestment risk" (or reward), though that shouldn't be your first consideration when deciding whether to buy them.

Unless you plan on holding a zero coupon bond until maturity, what should be the greatest concern of most investors is interest-rate risk. Most investors do not know that a zero coupon bond is approximately three times more volatile than a similar-type interest-bearing bond with a similar maturity. For example, a 30-year interest-bearing U.S. Government bond will fall approximately 8 percent (from, say, $1,000 to roughly $920) in value if interest rates rise a full point, whereas a similar 30-year zero coupon government bond will fall about 24 percent in value (from $1,000 down to roughly $760). (Note, though, that a full point rise rarely occurs at one time; instead, the Federal Reserve is likely to raise or lower interest rates in one-quarter- or one-half-point increments.)

Of course, if interest rates fall, the best bond to own is a 30-year zero coupon U.S. Government bond. A 1 percent drop means that the interest-bearing bond may have increased in value from $1,000 to roughly $1,080 (an approximate 8 percent increase). The zero coupon government bond, which was purchased for around $100, is now worth around $124 ($100 times a 24 percent increase). If ten zeros had been purchased for a total of $1,000 (to make the comparison equal), the ten zeros would be worth $1,240—quite an increase for a $1,000 investment in government securities.

Zero coupon bonds also carry some measure of financial risk. If you buy a zero coupon corporate or municipal bond with a maturity of ten, twenty or thirty years, there's no way of knowing how viable this entity will be when the bond matures. At least with an interest-bearing bond you are receiving interest every six months, and over the course of time, the cumulative interest payments are likely to exceed the original purchase price. With a zero coupon bond, on the other hand, if the bond goes into default prior to or at maturity, you get nothing. Fortunately, the chance of a highly rated zero coupon bond going into default or even becoming financially troubled is extremely remote.

Bond Funds

Instead of purchasing individual bonds, many investors find it easier to invest in bonds through mutual funds, which allow you to hold a more diversified bond portfolio and don't require a big investment. Bond funds are covered in more detail in the chapter on mutual funds, but here is a brief overview.

The typical bond fund has fifty to one hundred different issues with different maturities and different yields. These funds pay interest monthly, and any interest and gains can be automatically reinvested in the fund.

Fund choices correspond to most of the different types of bonds covered in this chapter. You can choose among government, corporate, or municipal funds, and within those categories you can select funds with short-term, intermediate-term, or long-term maturities. Additionally, there are funds that invest in federal agency issues, high-yield municipal and corporate bonds, foreign bonds, and emerging-markets bond funds. There are also global bonds, which invest in both U.S. and foreign bonds, and balanced funds, which invest in both stocks and bonds.

A major disadvantage of bond funds is that interest-rate risk generally remains constant. As bonds are sold or mature, they are replaced with new bonds that have a similar maturity to the rest of the portfolio. Funds are forced to do this because new money is almost always entering the fund and this new money (or reinvested interest payments) must be used to buy more bonds.

Your best bet is sticking to high-yield corporate and municipal bond funds or possibly foreign bond funds—funds that include securities that need to be closely monitored by professionals, the kind of monitoring you and I do not have the time, expertise, or staff to do. These types of bond funds also tend to have the best track records.

The Advantages of Bonds

Bonds are viewed as a conservative investment that provide a predictable income stream. Current yield helps to offset any losses from a drop in

Share the Pain

A large number of investors do not realize that Uncle Sam will share in your losses as well as your gains. If you sell a bond for a loss, you have what is known as a "realized loss" or "capital loss." Capital losses will offset capital gains (from any source), dollar for dollar, with no limit. If your gains are not as great as your losses, any excess loss can be used to offset what is referred to as "ordinary income" (income from salary, tips, bonuses, and commissions), up to $3,000 per calendar year. Any remaining excess loss can be carried forward to the next year. This carryforward can last indefinitely and is only lost when it is completely used up or at death.

bond prices and enhances total returns when bond prices climb. Historically, the return from bonds has been about half that of common stocks. Over the past fifty years, the worst fifteen-year period for medium-term government bonds provided an annualized return of just over 2 percent; the average for all fifteen-year periods was over 6 percent per year, while the best fifteen-year period resulted in average annual returns of over 11 percent. Contrast this with the S&P 500, whose worst such period was over 4 percent per year, 11 percent per year on average, and about 17 percent per year for the best fifteen-year period.

Though there have been extensive periods when long-term bonds have been more volatile than the S&P 500, bonds, on average, have about half the risk or volatility of stocks. Perhaps the biggest advantage of owning bonds is that there are usually few surprises. Unlike the stock market, the bond market does not drop 5 to 25 percent or more during the course of a couple of days or weeks. Volatility is sometimes greater on a daily basis, but when looking at a one-year or greater holding period, bonds are clearly the more conservative investment. And they can represent a safe haven when other investments are going down.

The Disadvantages of Bonds

Inflation is a bond's worst enemy. When you invest $10,000 in a ten- or twenty-year bond, you only get back $10,000 when the bond matures, even though the prices of goods and services have increased substantially over that ten- or twenty-year period. The purchasing power of that original $10,000 has dropped between 25 and 65 percent.

Of course, there are many other investments that have been even poorer hedges against inflation: gold, silver, oil, most other commodities, bank CDs, money market accounts, and U.S. Treasury bills. Bonds are the lesser of evils when it comes to debt instruments.

Which Bond Is Best for You?

Studies have shown that your return from a bond investment will most likely be whatever yield you are receiving. Bond values certainly go up and down, but overall this seems to have virtually no impact on the long-term investor. So your decision will depend upon what kind of current yield you need, as well as your risk level, time horizon, tax bracket, and current holdings. Here are some thoughts to guide you:

• For **maximum current income,** high-yield bond funds are your best choice.

What Matters

• Credit ratings, maturity, and yield-to-maturity.

• Comparison shopping for price.

• Including high-yield corporate or high-yield municipal bonds in your portfolio.

• Convertible securities as a *balance* between stocks and bonds.

What Doesn't

• Understanding the differences among government agency issues.

• Rating services other than S&P and Moody's.

• The difference between revenue and general obligation municipal bonds.

• Corporate bonds other than those rated below "investment grade."

• For **protection from interest-rate risk**, again, high-yield or short-term bond funds are your best choice.

• For the best **risk-adjusted returns**, intermediate-term bonds (ten-year maturity) are the best choice.

• If you believe **rates are going to fall**, buy bonds or a fund whose maturity is in the twenty-to-thirty-year range. Better yet, buy long-term zero coupon bonds; they are the most volatile of the entire bunch.

The longer your horizon, the more you can live with the ups and downs of longer-term bonds. Here are a few other criteria to keep in mind:

• If you are in a high or moderate tax bracket, stick with municipals.

• If the bonds are part of a qualified retirement account or within a variable annuity, go for the highest possible yield but still stick to maturities that you can live with.

• If a moderate or large portion of your portfolio is already in debt instruments, consider diversifying a little into a foreign or emerging markets bond fund or unit trust, depending upon your risk level.

Should You Own Bonds at All?

Conceptually, you should probably not own any bonds if your life expectancy is five to ten years or greater. This is because the S&P 500 has historically beat long-term U.S. Government bonds over the past half century (83 percent of the time for all five-year periods and 93 percent of the time for all ten-year periods). I emphasize the word "conceptually" because statistics are of little comfort to someone who invests in the stock market and then experiences a huge loss—one that may never be made up, either due to fear, a lack of patience, or owning speculative equities.

I have been an investment adviser specializing in equities for close to twenty years. Even though I have always been optimistic about the stock market as a whole and few, if any, things upset me, there have certainly been times when I wished that my entire portfolio were in bonds. So, although investors whose risk level is "moderate" or higher should probably not be in bonds, I recommend some bond exposure even for these people because emotions such as fear are much more powerful than historical trends and figures. By having a portion of your portfolio in bonds—anywhere from ten to thirty percent—you'll have money available that can go into the stock market after it has fallen five to ten percent or more.

THE BOTTOM LINE

Bonds have a place in most portfolios but should not be emphasized as much as what is recommended by the financial press or brokers. If top-quality bonds interest you, skip corporate issues and go right to U.S. Government securities. If you are in anything other than a lower tax bracket, municipal bonds are often a better alternative to governments and are far less volatile.

Historically, the best-performing bond category, at least on a before-tax basis, has been high-yield bonds. The best risk-adjusted returns are found with intermediate-term bonds. Finally, do not invest in domestic high-quality bond funds. You can do better on your own by avoiding their ongoing management fee and by tailoring a portfolio of individual quality securities to your particular needs.

CHAPTER 3

·····················

Trading Stocks

When a publicly traded company wants to raise capital, it can either borrow money (from a bank on a short-term basis or from issuing bonds on a long-term basis) or issue stock.

When you buy even a single share of a corporation's common or preferred stock, you become an owner of that company. You may only own 1/100,000 of 1 percent, but you are still an owner, and receive the same benefits as someone who owns a large chunk of the company, albeit relative to the percentage of the company that you own. You can vote on a wide range of issues relating to how the company is run, from electing the board of directors, who make long-term policy decisions, to hiring and firing senior management, such as the company's president and other executive officers. You participate in the corporation's earnings, either through dividends or as the value of the company and its shares grows.

In many respects, selling stock is the most painless way for a corporation to raise money, since there is no interest or principal to be paid back. And dividends can always be reduced or suspended—something that cannot be done with bond interest and principal payments unless the company wants court supervision or a shareholder revolt. Selling stock does mean more owners, though, and a greater dilution of profits.

Ways a Company Can Influence the Price of Its Stock

For the most part, the price per share of a stock is driven by the company's actions, the plans it announces, the earnings it reports, and the conclusions reached by stock analysts regarding such factors. The bottom line, as in any other business, is profitability, current as well as projected. Thus, a company may go through one or more quarters of flat sales and/or earnings, but still its stock may escalate in price because of analysts' and the public's excitement over the expected release of a new product or favorable research and development.

Besides being successful in the eyes of investors, a company can legally attempt to drive up the price of its own stock in one of three ways:

Buybacks

A corporation can buy back shares either through a tender offer, which is an announcement to buy a certain number of shares for a specific price, usually the current market price, or by buying on the open market. Either way, stock that is repurchased by the corporation is called "treasury stock." Even though money is being paid for these shares, they have no immediate value to the company. Treasury stock receives no dividends, and has no voting rights or other privileges afforded to other shareholders. Fortunately for the shareholders, treasury stock is not considered when the company calculates its earnings per share (EPS), and with fewer shares outstanding, the EPS of the company will be higher.

The company can distribute treasury shares to key employees or to workers at large through an employee stock option plan (ESOP). The corporation may also sell these shares back to the public at a later date. Once treasury shares are sold or distributed, they are just like any other shares of common stock.

Dividend Adjustment

Increasing the quarterly dividend is another way to influence the stock price. While shareholders benefit from increased cash flow, investors may or may not be concerned that the company is returning funds to shareholders that might better be used for research, expansion, advertising, incentives, and sales.

Stock Split

A stock split is the third way in which a company can focus attention on itself. Most stock splits are "2 for 1," meaning that existing shareholders as of a certain date will now own twice as many shares and each share will be worth one half of its then-current market value. Therefore, instead of owning one hundred shares worth $150 apiece, an investor would own two hundred shares worth $75 apiece. Whether the split is "2 for 1" or "3 for 2" or "1 for 2" (what is known as a "reverse split," since shareholders now own fewer shares but each share is worth more) the value of your investment does not increase or decrease.

More often than not, though, a stock will rise after the announcement of a split, and then again after the split. (There is always an interval of time between the announcement and the record date, which is when the split formally occurs.) Psychologically, investors like the idea of being able to buy more shares of stock for the same price. Small investors are attracted to lower-priced stocks since they feel that they are getting more bang for their buck.

Of course, there is no assurance that a split will lead to a price increase, and no way of gauging how much of stock's increase is due to a split and how much is due to other factors. A poor stock market, rising interest rates, troubled economic news, world conflict, and/or poor press surrounding a company can more than offset what would normally be considered a positive event. Nevertheless, most of the time, a stock split is generally considered to be good for the stock.

P/E Ratio

The P/E (price-earnings) ratio is more widely followed than EPS. The P/E ratio is calculated by taking the annual earnings of a company (on a per-stock share basis) and dividing it by its price per share. For example, if a company has a P/E of 15, this means that if you could buy 100 percent of the company tomorrow, it would take fifteen years to recoup your entire investment, based only on current earnings (not projected earnings which are almost always higher).

In general, the lower the P/E ratio, the more of a bargain the stock is; however, each industry group has its own average P/E ratio (e.g., high for technology and low for auto stocks) and any P/E ratio should be compared against its industry average to determine under- or overvaluation.

Where to Buy and Sell Stocks

All publicly traded stocks are listed on one or more exchanges or on the over-the-counter (OTC) market. From largest to smallest, the five major exchanges are the New York Stock Exchange

(NYSE), American Stock Exchange (AMEX) (located in New York City), Chicago Stock Exchange, Pacific Stock Exchange (located in San Francisco), and Boston Stock Exchange.

Combined, there are approximately six thousand stocks that trade on these exchanges. The most prestigious is the NYSE, where close to 75 percent of all exchange activity takes place. The AMEX is the second-largest exchange and accounts for about 20 percent of all exchange trading. The roughly remaining 5 percent is handled by the other exchanges.

With a few notable exceptions, the most widely held companies, such as AT&T, IBM, Boeing, General Electric, GM, Ford, and Exxon, are part of the more than four thousand common and preferred stocks that trade on the NYSE. Many of the largest foreign companies, such as Glaxo-Welcome, Gucci, Deutschebank, Shell Oil Company, and Telefonos de Mexico, also trade "on the big board," as it's called.

Each exchange sets its own listing requirements. The most stringent requirements are set by the NYSE. In order to get listed on one or more of the exchanges, certain criteria must be met regarding a company's before-tax earnings, the price of the security, the number of shareholders, the number of publicly held shares, plus the stock's daily average trading volume.

If a stock is not traded on an exchange, then it is traded over the counter (OTC). The OTC is not a formal exchange where brokers or specialists gather. Instead trades are performed by "market makers" across the country who have an inventory of the stock and/or stand ready to execute a trade either for their own account or for another client. The majority of OTC trades are made via a computerized system known as NASDAQ (National Association of Securities Dealers Automated Quotation system). The benefit of NASDAQ is that trades are executed more quickly and the investor receives the best possible price since the computer matches up the lowest seller with the highest buyer and vice versa.

Close to eighteen thousand stocks trade in the OTC market. Most of these stocks are small in comparison to those listed on the NYSE, but there are some notable exceptions. Microsoft and Intel are OTC stocks, and each has a market capitalization that is greater than more than 95 percent of the issues listed on any exchange.

The Indexes

The compensation of the majority of mutual fund managers is partly or largely based on performance. Management is rewarded for either outperforming its peer group (i.e., other growth funds or other government bond funds) or how it fares compared to a popular index or average. The best known average is The Dow Jones Industrial Average (the Dow). The best known index is the Standard & Poor's 500 (S&P 500).

The Dow is a price-weighted average of 30 very popular blue chip stocks, including IBM, McDonald's, Boeing, Walt Disney, Exxon, and General Motors. The Dow is the oldest and most widely quoted of all the market indicators. Other averages prepared by Dow Jones & Co. are the Dow Jones Transportation Average (twenty airline, trucking, railroad and shipping stocks) and the Dow Jones Utility Average (fifteen stocks of geographically representative gas and electric utility companies).

The S&P 500 is a market value-weighted index showing the change in the aggregate market value of 500 stocks (381 industrial stocks, forty-seven utilities, fifty-six financials, and sixteen transportation issues representing seventy to seventy-five percent of the market value of all stocks traded on the New York Stock Exchange (NYSE).

The Russell 2000 Small Stock Index is often used to compare the performance of fund managers who oversee a small company or aggressive growth fund. The Wilshire 5000 Equity Index is the broadest of all averages and indexes. It is market value-weighted and represents the value of all U.S. equities on the NYSE, American Stock Exchange (AMEX), and over the counter stocks tracked by the Value Line Investment Survey. The EAFE (Europe and Australia, Far East Equity index). This Morgan Stanley index acts as a benchmark for managers of foreign stock funds.

Types of Common Stock

There are at least ten different ways to categorize a common stock:

Blue Chip

Stocks of nationally known companies that have an extensive record of profit and dividend growth. These corporations are known and respected for their quality of product, services, and/or management. Examples include IBM, Microsoft, Intel, Boeing, GM, McDonald's, Gillette, and Exxon.

Countercyclical

Stocks that have a tendency to increase in price when the economy is in a recession or at least turning downward. Such companies are usually in industries whose product demand remains stable regardless of economic conditions. Examples include drugs, food, and tobacco.

Cyclical

Reactive stocks that can do particularly well when the economy is doing well and drop quite a bit when the economy is doing poorly. Examples of such industry groups include housing, autos, and paper.

Defensive

Stocks that are much less likely to suffer large losses when the market is doing poorly. Utility stocks are the prime example. Electric utility stocks have an average dividend of 5 percent (versus less than 6 percent for long-term U.S. Government bonds), and can act as a buffer to offset price depreciation. The industry group still remains largely monopolistic, and overseas problems have a minor impact on only a modest number of domestic utility companies.

Emerging Growth

Suitable for the aggressive investor, these are stocks from countries that are not considered financially or economically mature. A way to track these securities is by following the EMF (Emerging Markets Free) Index, developed by Morgan Stanley Capital International. The index includes the stock markets from the following countries: Argentina, Chile, Jordan, Malaysia, Mexico, the Philippines, and Thailand.

Established Growth

Stocks of companies that have been around for a number of years but are still showing steady increases in earnings and growth due to their growing market share. Examples of such companies include Coca-Cola, Gillette, and Microsoft.

Income

Stocks that pay high dividends, such as those of energy and utility companies, as well as real-estate investment trusts (REITs), insurance, and banking. Because dividends are taxable and considered "ordinary income," when given the choice, investors should shelter such stocks inside a qualified retirement account.

Interest Sensitive

Stocks of companies whose earnings are greatly affected when interest rates change. Bank and utility stocks are prime examples. Next to the price of energy, paying bond interest and stock dividends are the greatest expense of a utility company. When interest rates drop, so does the cost of debt, resulting in huge savings. For banks, when rates fall, the value of outstanding loans is at a premium (since the older loans are paying a comparatively higher rate). Banks also delay the lowering of rates they charge borrowers, thus benefiting from a wider spread when interest rates have fallen.

Penny

Stocks that sell for less than $1 per share and often represent companies that have a short or erratic track record. Most brokerage firms do not allow their brokers to solicit trades for stocks that trade for less than $5 a share. These stocks should be avoided.

Special Situation

Signified by stocks that fluctuate widely on a daily or weekly basis or undervalued stocks whose value is expected to increase over the next few weeks or months. The special situation may be the introduction of a new product, the realization of a large order, or a needed management change.

How to Buy a Stock

In order to buy or sell a stock, an order must be placed through a brokerage firm. Trades can be executed through full-service brokerage firms, discount brokerage firms, subsidiaries of banks, mutual funds, and insurance companies, or over the Internet. Most purchases and sales take place over the phone.

Types of Orders

The three most common types of orders are:

• Market

• Limit

• Stop

When you phone a broker and say, "Buy [or sell] two hundred shares of Chrysler," you are placing a **market order**. What makes it a market order is that you have not specified a price or specific time at which to make the trade. When your order reaches the exchange or is traded OTC within the next couple of minutes, it is bought (or sold) at the market price. The broker cannot guarantee a specific price on a market order, though there are other types of orders that can.

A **limit order** specifies the exact price at which you want the order executed. That price is always higher or lower than the market price when the order is entered. Limit orders are used by two types of investors: those who feel that they can get a slightly better price if they are a little patient, and those who want to sell at perhaps a significantly higher price and do not want to bother with tracking the stock on a day-to-day basis.

A **stop order**, also known as a **stop-loss**, is used when an investor wants to contain a loss or still walk away with some kind of profit. As with a limit order, a specified price is selected, but once that price is reached, the order becomes a market order and is executed at the then-best price. A stop order ensures that once the price is reached, the stock will then be sold. A limit order, on the other hand, does not turn into a market order; once the specific price is reached, it remains to be seen whether or not the order will be executed (e.g., just because the stock rises or falls to $25 a share does not mean that someone can buy or sell it at that exact price, or perhaps someone is willing to sell you one hundred shares at $25 but you want to buy fifteen hundred shares).

The best way to describe the difference between a stop order and a limit order is a stop order will automatically trigger a buy or a sell once the specified price is reached (the execution price could be this same price or a price that is slightly, or quite a bit, higher or lower than the "trigger"), whereas a limit order is more precise because a trade will only take place at the exact price, not even $\frac{1}{16}$ of a point higher or lower.

The vast majority of investors should use market orders. If you want to own a stock and it is trading at $40 a share, you could get tricky and place a limit order and try and buy it at $39.50 or some other figure, but if the stock starts to go up, it may never drop down to that $39.50 figure. You could end up missing a stock that skyrockets in value just because you were trying to save a few bucks. The same philosophy applies when you want to get out of a stock. If the stock has become a disappointment or you see a better opportunity elsewhere, you do not want to take the chance that the stock could fall even further, or you miss a different buying opportunity, just because the sell didn't take place at some price above its current market price.

I do recommend limiting orders for downside protection. This is a disciplined approach to get out of a stock and limit losses or, ideally, maintain some kind of profit on a security that was once at a much higher price. When a stock's price falls, investors can easily rationalize why they should stick with the stock (i.e., "It will turn around at this price" or "It can't get any lower than this" or "The stock's at a fifty-two-week low now, it's a good time to buy more shares"). I do not recommend limiting orders for the upside. Just because a stock has gone up 50 percent, 100 percent, or whatever your magical number is does not mean that the good times are about to end. In fact, probably the great majority of the money managers who are considered to be true experts, people such as John Templeton, Michael Price, and Peter Lynch, have greatly enhanced their track records by watching a 50 to 100 percent gain turn into a 200 to 400 percent gain.

SMART MONEY

I tell all of my clients that a broker, myself included, is not entitled to a full commission if the client has made the decision to buy or sell without any input or research on my part. If you trade through a full-service brokerage firm, you should only pay one half the standard commission unless your broker "earns" a full commission through research or intensive ongoing service.

In general, the reason I do not like limiting orders is that stocks often turn around and I want to be in that stock when it starts to perform well again. Furthermore, I want to reach my own conclusion on what I should do with the stock based on current news or some analysts' consensus. In short, I want to be more involved with the decision-making process, perhaps relying on late-breaking news instead of the mechanical process of a limit order.

Initial Public Offering

Those companies that do not already have publicly traded shares take themselves to the market by conducting an initial public offering (IPO). This is the first offering of common stock to the public. The public offering price, also known as the issue price, is set by the underwriter. Underwriters are investment bankers who are hired by the company going public. They advise the company as to the valuation of the stock, the number of shares that should be issued, and the price per share. Valuation is based on the company's current as well as projected sales, profits, market share, as well as on management and any patents, trademarks, and market niche. In addition, the investment bankers look at the value of other publicly traded companies in the same industry. Valuation is also based on a certain amount of intuitive judgment and underwriter experience as well as current market conditions.

IPO shares are all sold during a subscription period, which typically lasts thirty to sixty days. A "hot" IPO is one that is completely sold out in just a few days or less. It is usually large institutional buyers, such as brokerage firms, mutual funds, and pension plans, that end up with the vast majority of all highly desirable IPOs.

The purpose of a subscription period is to sell as many shares of the stock as possible. Sometimes an issue is "over subscribed," meaning that the buyers want to purchase more shares than are available, while other times a stock is not "fully subscribed" and any unsold shares are returned to the corporation. During the subscription period, all shares are sold for the same price. Large buyers pay the same price per share as individual investors. The level of interest in the IPO also has no effect on its price during the subscription period.

During the subscription period, shares can only be purchased—they cannot be sold. At the end of the period, market value is determined by the secondary market, which is either a formal exchange such as the New York Stock Exchange (NYSE) or over the counter (OTC). Once shares start to trade, the price per share is determined by investor expectations of the company's growth and earnings as well as any euphoria or disappointment surrounding the stock.

Strategies

Even though there has been an upward bias in the stock market for well over one hundred years, there have also been periods of time when one's patience has been tried. As shown by the following table, there have been eight periods since 1960 when the market, as measured by the Dow Jones Industrial Average, has fallen 20 percent or more.

Date	Drop	The Cause
1990	21.2%	Gulf War, interest rates raised in '88 and '89 recession
1987	36.1%	rates raised, dollar declines in value
1981–82	24.1%	rates raised, recession
1976–78	26.9%	rates raised, inflation rises
1973–74	45.1%	rates raised, first oil shock, inflation soars
1968–70	35.9%	rates raised, recession
1966	25.2%	rates raised
1961–62	27.1%	rates raised, Kennedy attacks steel price increase

Historically, most of these losses have been great enough and sustained enough to drive millions of investors out of stocks for at least several years. Drops since 1987 have been largely viewed as "buying opportunities," perhaps showing a trend that investors for the most part have become more patient or are at least more optimistic about the future of the overall market. Whatever the case, there are a number of strategies you can employ to reduce risk, increase profit potential, or even profit from market declines:

Buy and Hold

Without a doubt, this is the best strategy for most investors, living with the ups and the downs of the market: A well diversified stock portfolio is hard to beat. No financial guru, analyst, or brokerage firm can predict what the market will do tomorrow, much less next week or next year. A buy-and-hold strategy minimizes taxes (since you are only taxed on realized gains, meaning an actual sale) and transaction charges (no ongoing commissions and no bid-ask spreads), and makes tax preparation easier (only some dividend income to report each year).

Most important, patient stock investors who own a diversified portfolio have always been rewarded. Over time, no investment has done as well as common stocks, and it is doubtful that this will change in the future.

Dollar-Cost Averaging

This disciplined approach to investing works best with mutual funds but can be used with individual stocks as well. With dollar-cost averaging (DCA), a specific dollar amount is invested in the stock market each month, quarter, or year. The contribution continues regularly, regardless of which way the stock market is going.

Since there is a commission charge every time you buy shares of a stock, it may not be a good idea to make purchases every month. This is particularly true if you're investing a couple of hundred dollars. For example, a $30 commission charge on a $200 monthly purchase means that the stock must appreciate 15 percent before you break even ($30 / $200 = 15 percent). With no-load mutual funds, on the other hand, money can be added at any time without cost, fee, or commission.

DCA is a disciplined way to invest in the stock market because you are making a commitment to yourself to add to your portfolio on a regular basis, regardless of how you feel about the market's current conditions. DCA is also a way to invest a lump sum of money (e.g., large account balance in a checking account, inheritance, bonus, gift, etc.) over a period of time. Thus, someone who has $50,000 to invest in the stock market but is uncertain or nervous about current market conditions could invest $1,000 a month over the next fifty months, $5,000 per quarter for the next ten quarters, or whatever variation on this suits them.

If you have a lump sum to invest and are convinced that DCA is best for you, I strongly encourage you to spread out the investments over eighteen months or less. (A number of sources, including graduate business school texts, recommend a five-to-ten year horizon, but this is ridiculous. Over the past fifty years, the worst market has lasted about eighteen months—during the 1973–74 recession, when stocks dropped close to 50 percent. Using DCA to invest a lump sum over a period longer than eighteen months means you're speculating that the market may drop for more than eighteen months, something it has not done in over half a century.)

Constant-Dollar Plan

This strategy forces you to take profits out of the market when the price of a stock you own rises and to buy more shares when the stock declines. "Constant-dollar" means that you invest a lump sum of money in one or more stocks. Then, once a month or quarter, you look at the total value of the portfolio. If the value of the portfolio has declined in value, more money is added so that the value once again equals the original lump sum. If the portfolio has increased above the original principal, the increase is liquidated and the proceeds are put into a money market account.

The constant-dollar plan is simply a scaled-down version of the classic "buy low and sell high" philosophy. When there is a decline, you are buying into the market at a lower price. When there is an increase, you are selling off some shares at a higher price. This plan works best with stocks that are at least fairly volatile. (It would be ridiculous to buy and sell a stock that had a range of, say, $48 to $51.)

There are two disadvantages to the constant-dollar plan. First, every time there is a transaction, there will be a commission charge, though commissions can be eliminated by using mutual funds (which charge just $5 per transaction). Second, a tax event is triggered whenever something is bought or sold (there is a realized gain or loss). The only way to eliminate this disadvantage is to use this strategy with a sheltered vehicle such as a variable annuity (see chapter 5) or with a retirement account, such as an IRA, a Roth IRA, or a profit-sharing or 401(k) plan.

Constant-Ratio Plan

This is similar to the constant-dollar plan, but you are now dealing with percentages in a portfolio rather than dollar amounts. Here's how it works: If you have decided that you should have 70 percent in common stocks, 20 percent in bonds, and 10 percent in a money market account, then these percentage figures are constantly maintained. Once a month, quarter, or year, you tally up the value of your different holdings. Using the above percentages, if the stock portion has climbed from 70 percent to 73 percent, then 3 percent is sold off and divided up so that bonds stay at 20 percent and the money market stays at 10 percent (or whatever percentage breakdown you come up with for your portfolio).

Like constant-dollar, constant-ratio means that one part of the portfolio is sold at a high point, with the proceeds from the "excess" being invested in another segment at perhaps a lower price per share or unit. This "buy low and sell high" philosophy has the same potential problems as constant-dollar:

1. Transaction costs every time a trade occurs

2. Triggering a tax event whenever there is any kind of a sale

3. More complex and costlier tax preparation (since all sales must be listed on your return)

The constant-dollar and constant-ratio plans are designed for the long-term investor, and there is certainly no guarantee that by using either one you'll realize a gain. Always keep in mind, though, that whether you are using a ratio or fixed-dollar figure, the higher the percentage of the portfolio devoted to equities (common stocks), the greater the risk level.

Margin Account

The vast majority of brokerage accounts are referred to as "cash accounts," meaning that you pay for the securities after a purchase is made. A margin account, on the other hand, allows you to borrow money from the brokerage firm. The money borrowed can be used for anything you like: The brokerage firm can send you a check for the amount borrowed or you can use the leverage in a margin account to buy more securities. This use of leverage gives you more bang for the buck since you can double the value of the securities in the account. If cash is sent to you, then the typical limit is 50 percent of the value of the account.

For example, suppose you had an account that was worth $50,000. By using margin, you could either have a check for $25,000 sent to you or you could buy up to $50,000 worth of additional securities (you would then have an account that contained $100,000 worth of securities, but you would also owe the brokerage firm $50,000). Whatever you borrow, either as cash or to make additional purchases, is what you owe the brokerage firm— plus interest. The brokerage firm charges you interest because you are using their money. The interest rate charged is usually 1 to 2 percent higher than the prime rate, but the more you borrow (or margin), the lower the interest rate. Other than the interest, there are no costs or fees to start, maintain, or terminate a margin agreement.

Brokerage firms like margin agreements for a few reasons. First, they are charging you interest. Second, many people use their margin accounts to buy more securities, which, in turn, generates more commissions for the brokerage firm. Finally, the account represents a low-risk loan for the brokerage firm because the firm holds on to your securities as collateral. If the account increases in value, so can the collateral. The client can pretty much buy and sell anything, but the new or existing positions remain in the account as collateral.

Investors, too, are attracted to these types of accounts for several reasons. First, it is a way to pull money out of your account immediately (once the margin agreement has been signed and approved) without paying any points or origination fees or going through a qualification process. Second, if the money is used to purchase more securities, the overall rate of return can be substantially higher than it would be if buying the securities with cash, since with a margin account you are using borrowed money (leveraging your profits). Third, you do not have to directly pay any interest charges. Interest is computed daily and simply debited from the account's "purchasing power." Interest charges could literally accrue indefinitely without your ever having to write a check. As long as the accrued interest plus the amount of the loan do not exceed a certain percentage of the account's value (which is set by each brokerage firm but generally ranges from 50 to 70 percent of the account), you have sufficient collateral.

For investors, a margin account also has some negatives. First, the debit in the account increases slightly each day because you are being charged interest. This is a real expense, even though you are not writing a check to cover it. Second, if the account drops in value, then leverage changes from your best friend to your worst enemy. A regular account that drops 10 percent is not nearly as bad as the same account on margin dropping 10 percent because with the margin account the loss is twice as great since you have doubled your positions. And, on top of any loss, you are still incurring interest charges.

Setting up a margin account is an excellent

idea for anyone who needs money and their only other option would be to sell off securities in a brokerage account, assuming the rate of return on the securities portfolio is higher than the interest rate being charged. If you margin a bond account that yields 6 percent and you are incurring a 7 to 9 percent interest charge, then margining is a bad idea. If, instead, the account has been averaging 12 to 15 percent a year, then margining it is a good way for you to get the needed cash.

Leveraging your investment purchasing power is a strategy only recommended for investors whose risk level is at least moderate; an aggressive investor is an even more appropriate candidate. I say "moderate" because, historically, someone who margined a broad-based portfolio, say one whose performance was similar to the S&P 500 Index, did much better than someone who had just a cash account (no leverage). The reason for this is simple: Over the past one, three, five, ten, fifteen, twenty, and twenty-five years, the overall growth rate of the stock market has been greater—sometimes substantially greater—than whatever the then-current interest rate being charged on a margin account.

SMART DEFINITION

Capitalization Ratio
One measure used to evaluate an investor's risk level is the corporation's capitalization ratio, which shows what percentage of the total is debt (bonds and notes), preferred stock, and common stock.

Short Selling

Although it's a practice viewed as almost "un-American," you can make money on the stock market when it is going down by "shorting" it. When you short a stock, you are betting that the stock is going to drop in value between the date on which you short the stock and the day on which you cancel out the short (known as "buy back" the stock). A short sale means that you are selling something you do not own. Let's go through an example to see how short selling works.

Suppose you are convinced that LMN stock, which currently trades at $60 a share, is going to fall. You contact your broker and tell her you want to "short two hundred shares of LMN stock." The brokerage firm then sells two hundred shares of LMN at the market price. At some time in the future you decide to "close out the position" by buying two hundred shares of LMN stock at the then-market price. You need to buy the shares so that you can make the brokerage firm whole again (since they lent you the shares to sell). If the short sale was for $60 a share and you bought the stock a week (or a month, year, etc.) later at $45 a share, you will have a profit of $3,000 ($15 x 200). If, instead, LMN is bought back at a higher price than the short-sale price, there will be a loss (e.g., you buy it for $80 a share, so you end up losing $20 a share).

Short selling can be a very aggressive strategy since your upside potential is fixed (the price of the stock can't go below 0), but your downside potential is unlimited (the stock could go up to several hundred dollars per share). Since shares are being borrowed, a short sale can only take place in a margin account. Losses (the price of the stock goes up instead of down after the short sale) or gains can be limited because you can buy back the shares of stock you sold short at any time. Because of the potentially large losses, the lengthy discussion involved with explaining short selling to clients, plus the idea that you are not being patriotic (after all, you are hoping that a company drops in value), short selling is not a strategy used by the vast majority of investors.

Analyzing Stocks

Two of the most popular ways to analyze a stock are fundamental analysis and technical analysis.

Fundamental Analysis

A "fundamentalist" looks at general economic conditions or financial information about the specific company under review. General economic conditions include such things as interest rates, inflation, unemployment, business inventories, and changes in the gross national product (GNP). The analyst is looking for indications of overall positive (bullish) or negative (bearish) signs. The conclusion reached will help determine whether stocks should be bought or sold.

It has often been said that you invest in a market of stocks, not the stock market (meaning excellent gains can be obtained with some stocks even when the overall market is going down). Fundamental analysis is more concerned with a company's financial statements as a means of forecasting the stock's future price. Such analysis looks at assets, earnings, sales, products, management, and competing markets. The conclusion reached by the fundamentalist is that the stock is undervalued (a buy recommendation), overvalued (a hold or sell recommendation), or fairly priced (a hold or accumulate recommendation).

Technical Analysis

The "technician" is mostly concerned with the price and volume movements of stocks. By studying a market's or stock's past movement (i.e., increasing or decreasing volume along with increasing or decreasing prices), technical analysis hopes to be able to predict future trends. Technicians are also referred to as "chartists" since they heavily rely on different types of charts (which show daily, weekly, and/or monthly changes in volume and price).

Technical analysis believes that history repeats itself. The hope is that past movements will repeat themselves in the future. As an example, if past patterns show that when there is growing volume (interest in the stock), the price of the stock will shortly thereafter start to rise, the technician wants to see such volume patterns begin to repeat themselves—thereby indicating a "buy" signal.

Technical analysis also often includes "sentiment indicators" and "flow of funds indicators." "Sentiment" looks at whether the majority of investors and/or analysts feel bullish or bearish

Track Record: Popular Indices

Here are annualized returns for periods ending June 30, 1998, for a broad range of indices and averages:

Index or Average	3-year %	5-year %	10-year %	15-year %
S&P 500 (large cap. stocks)	30.2	23.1	18.6	17.2
Russell 2000 (small cap. stocks)	18.9	16.1	13.6	11.1
MSCI EAFE (foreign stocks)	10.7	10.0	6.8	15.1
Lehman Bros. bond (all bonds)	7.9	6.9	9.1	10.2
First Boston High-Yield Bonds	11.9	10.4	11.6	n/a
Lehman Bros. Corp. Bond (U.S.)	8.4	7.5	9.8	10.9
Lehman Bros. Gov't Bond (U.S.)	7.7	6.7	8.9	9.9
Lehman Bros. Municipal Bond	7.9	6.5	8.3	9.4
Non-U.S. World Gov't Bond	0.4	6.4	8.2	n/a

about the market. Such a consensus view is reached by polling investment newsletters. More often than not, the technician concludes the opposite of what these investment advisory services publish. It is believed that the consensus is wrong, and therefore sentiment is usually considered to be a "contrary" indicator (going in the opposite direction of the masses).

"Flow of funds indicators" look at how individuals and institutions are investing their money. If lots of money is pouring into the stock market, it is considered a bullish sign for stocks. Similarly, if money is flowing out of bond funds, it is considered a bearish sign for bonds. You can learn more about the flow of funds by looking at where people are investing their mutual fund money and through periodic surveys of pension fund managers.

Dow Theory

A form of technical analysis, the Dow Theory believes that a major upward or downward trend in the stock market must be confirmed by a similar trend in the DJIA and the Dow Jones Transportation Average. Unless both the Industrial Average and the Transportation Average reach new highs or lows, the theory believes that the market will go back to its former trading range. Unfortunately, even if one believes in this theory, there is no universal agreement as to when the chart pattern is indicating a true "breakout" (meaning a new trend or direction in the market).

The Advance-Decline Theory

This theory looks at the number of stocks that have advanced for the day versus the number of stocks that have declined. In the "Diaries" section

WHAT MATTERS, WHAT DOESN'T

What Matters

- Stocks of established companies, particularly blue-chips.

- Discount and Internet brokerages.

- Buy-and-hold unless the fundamentals have changed.

- Fundamental analysis.

- Changes in interest rates.

What Doesn't

- Technical analysis, particularly after a large market decline.

- IPOs and penny stocks—both tempting but dangerous.

- Dollar-cost averaging unless you are conservative or undisciplined.

- The different stock theories—newspapers need to fill their pages each day.

- Short-term swings in the stock market.

of the *Wall Street Journal* is a table that shows the number of advances and declines for the NYSE, AMEX, and NASDAQ. By plotting the daily net advances or declines (subtracting one from the other) on graph paper, technicians look for a positive (the number of advances is increasing) or negative (the number of declines is increasing) trend.

The Random Walk Theory

This theory states that all stock analysis, whether technical or fundamental, is of no value. The theory believes that a stock's price, as well as the overall direction of the market, is unpredictable, at least in the short run. The investor can select stocks at random, and, over the long term, a well diversified, blindly selected portfolio should do just as well as a portfolio made up of analysts' recommendations.

On a regular basis, the *Wall Street Journal* tests this theory by pitting a handful of stock "experts" against stocks selected by *Journal* employees tossing darts at a large page of listed and OTC stocks. There is always a clear winner, but no clear winner over time.

CHAPTER 4

....

Investing through Mutual Funds

Though many people think of mutual funds as a recent invention, they were created almost 150 years ago and have been available in the United States since the early 1920s. As of the middle of 1998, there were more than ten thousand different funds in this country, with a total investment of $5 trillion in the United States alone.

A mutual fund is a type of investment company. When you buy shares in a mutual fund, you are an owner of the company's investment portfolio, not the company itself.

Unlike stocks, whose value changes throughout the trading day (Monday through Friday, excluding certain holidays), a mutual fund's price per share, also called the net asset value (NAV), is calculated only at the end of each trading day. The total market value of all the securities owned by the fund is divided by the number of outstanding shares. For example, if the XYZ Fund was worth $200 million on Tuesday morning and there were 50 million shares of the XYZ Fund, the price per share would be $4 (200 million divided by 50 million). When an investor buys shares of the fund, if there is a difference between the purchase price and the NAV, then the investor is paying an up-front commission (see page 94).

The Best Things about Mutual Funds

People, institutions, and retirement plans invest in mutual funds for one or more of the following reasons:

1. Convenience. Mutual fund investments are easy to make: You call your broker and buy X dollars' worth of the ABC Growth Fund or you send a check and application directly to the fund. Confirmation of the purchase automatically follows. You can track the performance of your mutual fund just as easily, by looking up the price per share in the mutual fund listings in the business section of your newspaper or by calling the mutual fund company (almost all of them have toll-free numbers).

2. Professional management. A dedicated manager or team makes all of the investment decisions, based on their evaluation of specific securities, the economy, interest rates, competing investments, and world events. This means your investment is being monitored throughout the day. Management also relies on and works with research analysts, who are constantly reviewing reports as well as actually visiting companies. These personal visits help management gain more intimate knowledge about a company and its top personnel. Additionally, professional managers have extensive experience with the ups and downs of the marketplace, and are much likelier to invest with dispassionate objectivity rather than in reaction to fear, greed, or instinct (unlike individual investors, who are often shortsighted and swayed by recent market activity, news reports, seminars, or financial "gurus").

3. Risk reduction. A portfolio of several dozen securities, representing a number of different industry groups, bought at different prices and times, possesses much less risk than one comprising just a handful of stocks and/or bonds. Many studies have shown that a portfolio with just two to

F.Y.I.

Unlike with individual stocks or bonds, the price per share of a mutual fund has nothing to do with whether or not the securities in its portfolio are at an all-time high, low, or average. A fund that sells for $100 a share is not a better bargain than one that sells for $7 a share. Instead, the fund's price per share is largely determined by the number of outstanding fund shares.

five stocks is several times riskier than a portfolio with fifty stocks, without any potential for greater return. Individual investors rarely have the time to research and track such a broad portfolio, nor do they generally have sufficient resources to purchase so many different securities—thus, the appeal of mutual funds.

At any point in time, the stock market will naturally favor certain sectors (or industry groups) and dislike others. The market may favor an area because it is experiencing tremendous growth (computers) or large profit margins (software and pharmaceuticals), or because it has captured Wall Street's imagination (biotechnology). Certain stocks or industry groups may fall out of favor for several weeks, months, or even years due to depressed sales, poor growth, or slim profit margins.

Since no one can predict what the market will favor tomorrow, much less next week, month, or year, owning a wide range of stocks means that you have a good chance of having some strong winners. It also means that some of your stocks will be underperformers at any given time, but this is often not significant because most stocks go up in value over time.

4. Multiple features. Mutual funds also offer a wide array of features, including:

• **Exchange privileges.** You can move your money from one fund to another within the same "family" at a cost of $5.

• **Liquidity.** You can increase your investment or withdraw money easily at any time. And when you do so, it doesn't imbalance your portfolio.

How Volatile Is Your Fund?

The most common measure of mutual fund risk is its "standard deviation," or range of returns. Most mutual fund sources provide this figure, which measures the fluctuations (range of returns) in a fund's performance over the prior thirty-six months.

The higher the standard deviation, the greater the range of returns—and therefore, the more volatile the fund. Unlike past performance figures, which are rarely an indicator of future results, standard deviation is a pretty reliable indicator of future volatility. The following chart indicates the average standard deviations by category of fund:

Category	Standard Deviation %
Money market	1
Government bonds	7
High-yield bonds	9
Convertibles	10
Balanced	10
Global bonds	10
Small company	12
Growth	12
Equity-income	12
Growth and income	13
Utilities	13
Aggressive growth	13
International stock	17
Emerging markets	33
Precious metals	41

Growth funds, for example, which had an average annual return of 14 percent for the past five years, have a standard deviation of 12 percent. This means that over the next two out of three years, the range of returns you should expect is 14 percent (its average annual return) plus or minus 12 percent (26 percent to 2 percent). As you can see, money market funds are the most stable category by a wide margin, while emerging markets and precious metals are clearly the most volatile.

• **Income.** Interest from bond or money market funds can be sent to you monthly.

• **Systematic withdrawal plan (SWP).** You can have a set dollar amount sent to you each month, quarter, or year, regardless of market performance (some shares of your fund are redeemed each period).

• **Dollar-cost averaging (DCA).** This is an easy way to slowly move into the stock and/or bond markets. Part or all of your investment dollars can be initially invested in a conservative fund, such as a money market or short-term bond fund, and then invested in more aggressive funds in even increments each month. For more information on DCA, see pages 71–72.

• **Easier tax preparation.** By using the year-end summary statement, which shows all buys, sells, dividends, interest payments, and/or capital gains paid during the calendar year, shareholders can quickly determine any tax liability.

• **Toll-free telephone number.** Fund representatives are available to answer questions about fund holdings, historical performance, risk level, any upcoming tax considerations, plus other funds offered by the same fund family.

• **The ability to track day-to-day price changes.** Most newspapers have a mutual fund section that alphabetically lists the name of the fund family in boldface type and then lists each member of the fund family, showing its price per share and how much the fund lost or gained the previous day.

• **Low transaction costs.** Several thousand funds do not charge a purchase or redemption fee (also referred to as a "load" or "commission").

• **Economies of scale.** Because they are dealing with such large amounts of money, funds' buy and sell costs are a fraction of what most investors pay.

• **Accountability.** Unlike stockbrokers and financial planners, funds have track records that can be verified. There are a number of independent sources, including the *Wall Street Journal, Barron's, Forbes,* Morningstar, and *Value Line,* that track performance on a daily, weekly, and/or monthly basis.

• **Retirement accounts.** IRAs, Roth IRAs, Keoghs, and 401(k) plans are just some of the qualified retirement accounts you can set up through a mutual fund at minimal cost.

5. Performance. Mutual funds provide a level of returns that only a very small percentage of individuals can match, even when those funds don't beat the common industry benchmarks, known as indexes (for more information, see pages 61–62 in chapter 3), such as the S&P 500.

In part this is because there are costs associated with running a mutual fund (i.e., printing and sending out literature, personnel, research, paying for top management, fees associated with the buying and selling of securities, rent, advertising, etc.). Furthermore, even though the vast majority of funds underperform the indices, in many cases these funds maintain a lower risk level than that of the marketplace they focus on, and these "underperformers" may therefore have better risk-adjusted returns than a fund that mimics the S&P 500 or some other index.

Tracking Performance

As previously mentioned, most newspapers track the performance of several thousand mutual funds daily. The example and accompanying text below is from the *Wall Street Journal*, but your newspaper's format should be very similar.

Mutual fund quotations are in the business section of your newspaper. Once you have found this section, look for the name of the fund family listed alphabetically in boldface type. Under the fund family name (e.g., Fidelity, Oppenheimer, Vanguard, etc.) look for the name of the fund you are interested in; the names of the funds within the family are often abbreviated and they are also listed alphabetically.

Fund Name	Bid	Ask	Net Change
Blockworth Group			
Bond	1.57	1.57	0.02
Enterp	20.15	20.15	0.12
Gwth	20.83	20.83	-0.07

This example shows the Blockworth Group of mutual funds. The family consists of three funds: Bond, Enterprise, and Growth. The newspaper abbreviation is such that we cannot tell whether or not the bond fund is corporate, government, or municipal. Enterprise is probably some type of stock fund, but it could be another type of fund. Growth is most likely a U.S. stock fund that invests in growth stocks. Owners of these different funds will know what they own and can determine which fund listing applies to them.

Using "Bond" as our more detailed example, we see that the price per share is $1.57 and that there is no up-front commission (since the "bid" and the "ask," also known as the "buy" and "sell," prices are the same). We also see that the price per share has increased by two cents from the previous day ("net change").

The Prospectus

The prospectus is a formal written document filed with the Securities and Exchange Commission (SEC) that sets forth a fund's objective, track record, expenses, and sales charge (if any), as well as the history and background of its managers. Funds are required to update the prospectus at least once every thirteen months. New investors must be given a prospectus at or prior to the time of purchase. The table of contents below from one of the Franklin Funds will give you a good idea as to the information contained in the prospectus.

- Expense Summary

- Financial Highlights

- How the Fund Invests Its Assets

- The Fund's Potential Risks

- Who Manages the Fund

- How Performance Is Measured

- The Effects of Taxation

- The Fund's Organization

- How You Buy and Sell Shares

- Exchanging Shares

- Distributions

- Services to Help You

- Account Registration

- How and When Shares Are Priced

- Share Certificates

- Phone Numbers for Questions

- Glossary of Terms and Definitions

The most important sections of the prospectus are the expense summary, how to buy and sell shares, how the fund invests its assets (the investment objective), and who manages the fund.

Expense Summary

Every fund incurs a variety of costs associated with buying, selling, and owning shares of the fund. The Expense Summary does not include or reflect any of the costs of buying or selling securities. For example:

- **Management fees** compensate the fund company for running the fund.

- **Rule 12b-1 fees** are charged to offset some of the fund's marketing and promotional expenses. (In other words, they charge you for their advertising.) Well over half the funds out there have such a hidden annual fee, which typically ranges from 0.25 to 1.25 percent.

These fees make up a fund's total operating expense, which is expressed as a percentage figure, called the expense ratio. The lower the expense ratio, the greater the return to you—in other words, the more you get to keep of what the fund earns. If a fund states that its return for the year was 18 percent and its expense ratio is 1.6 percent, the real return was 19.6 percent—but shareholders actually receive only 18 percent.

Since the expense ratio has a lot to do with the long-term performance of a fund, you'll want to know how any given fund's ratio compares to that of other funds within the same category. Here are the average expense ratios by category, as of June 30, 1998:

Aggressive growth	1.7%
Balanced	1.4%
Corporate bond	0.9%
Equity-income	1.3%
Government bond	1.1%
Growth and income	1.3%
Growth	1.5%
High-yield bond	1.4%
International stock	1.9%
Municipal bond	1.0%
Small company	1.5%

How to Buy and Sell Shares

This section of the prospectus will tell the minimum initial investment (usually $250 to $1,000), the minimum additional investment (usually $25 or $50), and, most important, the costs associated with any purchase.

A fund that charges no commission up front or upon redemption is known as a **no-load fund.** A fund that charges an initial or possible back-end penalty is called a **load fund**. A **low-load fund** has a commission charge of 3 percent or less.

The majority of funds charge a commission, but there are literally thousands that do not. Whether or not you should pay a commission depends upon the kind of advice or service you are given by a broker or your financial adviser. Good advice is easily worth any sales charge; however, in general, a fund that charges a commission does not perform any better than one that does not.

Load funds can work in a number of different ways, by offering what are known as A, B, or C shares.

• **A shares,** called a front-end load, have an upfront sales charge (sometimes referred to as a commission). The disadvantage of A shares is that the fee comes off the top immediately; it is money that is not invested in the fund. For example, if you invest $10,000 in the XYZ Bond Fund and that fund charges a 3 percent commission, only $9,700 is actually being invested. The other $300 (which is 3 percent of $10,000) is a commission charge that goes into the broker's pocket. Most front-end funds charge a commission that ranges from 3 to 5 percent.

• **B shares,** also referred to as a back-end load, have no initial charge, but there is a surrender fee if the shares are redeemed within a certain time period (typically from five to seven years). Most funds also levy an additional 1 percent annual charge to such accounts (this fee is hidden but certainly affects the net performance).

• **C shares** have no up-front commission and no back-end charges if the investor stays within the same family of funds for a minimum period of time (usually twelve to eighteen months). As with B shares, most funds also levy an additional 1 percent annual charge to such C-share accounts (again, this fee is hidden but certainly affects the net performance).

How the Fund Invests Its Assets

This section describes, in very general terms, what the fund can and cannot invest in. It also indicates whether or not aggressive trading techniques (i.e., leveraging the fund by borrowing money, dealing in futures contracts or options, etc.) are used. Management must always stay within the confines of the investment objective. Since most funds want to give their managers fairly broad latitude, the wording of this section is not particularly concise. Still, it remains the best part of the prospectus for at least getting a rough idea as to the potential risks of investing in the fund.

The following is not something you will find in any prospectus. It is my interpretation as to what the fund actually means when it describes its investment objective.

What the Fund Says
Large Cap Value
What It Means
Stocks of companies that are less expensive than the market as a whole, as measured by the S&P 500 (whose average stock has a market capitalization of approximately $30 billion). The out-of-favor stocks and/or slow growers selected tend to pay relatively high dividends. Selection often comes from the following industry groups: utilities, energy, and cyclical sectors. Largest holdings of these funds are Philip Morris, Mobil, IBM, Ford, and Bristol-Myers Squibb.

What the Fund Says
Large Cap Growth
What It Means
Blue-chip stocks whose P/E multiples are typically higher than those of S&P 500 stocks. The companies selected tend to have a long history of somewhat predictable growth. Favored selections include large multinationals and technology companies. Largest holdings of these funds are Intel, GE, Pfizer, Microsoft, and Merck.

What the Fund Says
Mid-Cap Value
What It Means
Stocks of all sizes, but predominantly those whose market value ranges from $1 to $5 billion. These funds invest in all sectors, trying to find comparatively inexpensive equities. Largest holdings of these funds are Chase Manhattan, RJR Nabisco, Philip Morris, Owens-Illinois, and IBM.

What the Fund Says

Mid-Cap Growth

What It Means

Predominantly stocks whose market value ranges from $1 to $5 billion but have higher-than-average P/E ratios. The favorite sector of this group is technology issues; smaller-cap stocks from a wide range of industry groups are also favored. Performance tends to more closely match small-cap stock indices instead of the S&P 500. Largest holdings of these funds are HFS, Microsoft, BMC Software, WorldCom, and Computer Associates.

What the Fund Says

Small-Cap Value

What It Means

Stocks whose market capitalization is under $1 billion. Concentration is on cheap stocks that are "undiscovered" or those whose companies have management or growth problems. Favorite industry groups are industrials, financial, services, and technology. Largest holdings of these funds are Enhance Financial Group, Quanex, XRE, Sierra Health Services, and Bowne.

What the Fund Says

Small-Cap Growth

What It Means

Stocks whose market capitalization is under $1 billion. The focus is on stocks of rapid-growth industries such as the Internet, software, networking, and medical-device issues. Largest holdings of these funds are Concentra Managed Care, Applied Graphics Technologies, Network Appliance, American Disposal Services, and Signature Resorts.

What Matters

- Annual returns.

- How a fund compares to its peer group.

- Management with at least five years' experience running the fund.

- Risk-adjusted returns.

- Not paying a commission—unless you are getting valuable advice.

What Doesn't

- Weekly, monthly, or quarterly returns.

- Price per share.

- How a fund compares to the entire mutual fund universe.

- Magazine "top ten" or "best-performing" lists.

- Tax consequences from distributions for equity funds—the whole issue is over-rated.

What the Fund Says
Convertibles
What It Means
Offers some of the appreciation potential of common stocks while also supplying one half to three quarters of the income of a high-quality bond portfolio. These funds typically have 65 percent of their holdings in convertibles (a security that can be converted into a common stock), 10 percent in common stocks, 10 percent in regular bonds, and the balance in cash and "other." The average quality rating of the securities in these portfolios is BB, just below investment grade.

What the Fund Says
Balanced
What It Means
These funds invest in common stocks, bonds, convertibles, and cash. In general, roughly 40 to 65 percent is in stocks, with most of the balance in investment-grade bonds. Financial, cyclicals, technology, and services dominate the stock side. Approximately 10 percent of the stock portfolio is often invested in foreign stocks.

What the Fund Says
Emerging Markets
What It Means
Stocks from companies in developing markets such as Brazil, Mexico, South Africa, India, Thailand, and Argentina. These high-risk, high-reward funds are also concerned with currency swings (how the country's currency fares against the U.S. dollar). Appreciation (e.g., fewer pesos to equal $1) against the dollar adds to a portfolio's return, while depreciation (e.g., more pesos to equal $1) harms returns.

What the Fund Says

Foreign Stock

What It Means

Funds can invest anywhere in the world except in the United States. The greatest exposures are in Japan, the U.K., France, the Netherlands, and Germany. These funds have little, if any, exposure to emerging markets. Performance of this group is usually compared to the MSCI EAFE Index or the MSCI World ex-U.S. Index.

What the Fund Says

World Stock

What It Means

These funds can invest anywhere, and typically have 30 to 45 percent of their holdings in U.S. stocks. The U.K., Japan, France, and Germany are the next most common areas of investment, but the exposure to each of these countries is frequently 2 to 10 percent of the entire portfolio. Due to their wide geographical diversification, these funds are almost always less risky than a pure foreign stock fund and sometimes less volatile than a U.S.-only stock portfolio.

What the Fund Says

Long-Term Government

What It Means

Bond funds that invest in U.S. Treasury bonds and notes plus agency issues such as GNMA and FNMA. Typical maturity of these "AAA+"-quality portfolios is fifteen to seventeen years. These funds will increase about 3 to 4 percent in value when interest rates fall 1/2 percent and drop 2 to 3 percent in value when rates increase by 1/2 percent. Investors should figure that total return (yield plus appreciation or minus depreciation of principal) will, long-term, equal current yield.

What the Fund Says

Intermediate-Term Government

What It Means

Bond funds that invest in GNMAs, FNMAs, and U.S. Treasury bonds and notes. Typical maturity of these "AAA+"-quality portfolios is seven to ten years. These funds have about half the interest-rate risk of their long-term brethren.

What the Fund Says

Short-Term Government

What It Means

Bond funds that invest in money market instruments, GNMAs, FNMAs, and U.S. Treasury notes. Typical maturity of these "AAA+"-quality portfolios is three to five years. These funds have very little interest-rate risk or reward. Return, or yield, is about ½ percent higher than that of a bank CD or money market account. These are very conservative funds.

What the Fund Says

High-Yield

What It Means

Bond funds that invest in below-investment-grade issues; bonds rated BB and B are highly favored; Average maturity is 5 to 9 years. These funds have less interest-rate risk than their government bond fund counterparts but much more financial risk. The default rate for junk bonds is about 1 percent a year; less than one half this figure with professionally managed funds.

What the Fund Says
Municipal Bond
What It Means
Bond funds that invest in bonds issued by state and local governments and their agencies. Interest from these funds is exempt from federal income taxes. Realized gains (from capital gains or the sale or exchange of shares at a profit) are fully taxable. The average credit quality rating is a high AA. If the word "national" appears in the fund's title, you will be paying state income taxes on the interest (current yield). If the name of your state of residence appears in the fund's name, then no state (or federal) taxes are due on the interest received or reinvested. Like government bond funds or high-quality corporate bond funds (which are not included in these descriptions since they are highly similar to government securities of a comparable maturity), municipal bond funds come in three maturity ranges: short-, intermediate-, and long-term. Intermediate-term funds have the best risk-adjusted returns.

Who Manages the Fund

The portfolio management section of the prospectus details the educational background and experience of the person or people who oversee the daily buying and selling for the fund. Essentially, when you are buying a fund, you are buying the talents of the managers. As a prospective investor, you want to look for managers with a history of managing the same or similar securities as those of the fund they're currently managing. It is of no comfort or benefit, for example, to have a growth fund being managed by a someone whose

SMART MONEY

For most investors, subscribing to a number of different investment services, newspapers, newsletters, or magazines can be both time consuming and confusing, time consuming (e.g., do you buy or sell a fund that is recommended by one source but disliked by another?). My recommendation is, do not subscribe to newsletters.

With hundreds of newsletters to choose from, there will always be a few hot ones, but there is truly no relationship between their track record of recommendations and what will occur in the future—and anyway, their overall track record is not very good. And the more expensive newsletters are not any better than the cheaper ones.

background is in bonds or emerging markets. You also want to see how long the manager has been running the fund.

Recommended Funds

Listed below are specific funds that are considered to be some of the very best, along with a brief description of what I like about these funds. All of the selections below are from *The 100 Best Mutual Funds You Can Buy,* a book I write each year. The list is drawn from funds that have had the same management for at least the last five years (this single criterion eliminates more than half the field). There are so many excellent seasoned money managers to choose from that I don't see any need to take chances by relying on a short-term record.

My other selection requirements are equally straightforward and simple:

• The risk level must be below the average for the category (since growth funds, for example, have a different average risk level than aggressive growth funds).

• Returns must be higher than the average for the category.

• Risk-adjusted returns must be excellent (e.g., a fund may have only slightly better-than-average returns but a risk level that is one half the category's average—this would be an example of excellent risk-adjusted returns). My selections emphasize risk-adjusted returns more than other "best" lists.

High Risk

Baron Asset
800-992-2766
- Very high return potential with average risk for an "aggressive growth" fund

- Excellent tax minimization, particularly during bull markets

- Only one negative year during the past decade (18 percent in 1990)

- Up 35 percent in 1995, the fund's best year so far

Longleaf Partners Small-Cap
800-445-9469
- High return potential yet has been safer than 95 percent of its peers

- Good tax minimization (93 percent of gains are retained)

- Worst year since inception was 1990 (-30 percent) and best year so far was 1989 (+34 percent); superb risk-adjusted returns

Winthrop Small Company Value
800-225-8011
- Has outperformed 80 percent of all other funds and has been safer than 88 percent of them

- Tax minimization has only been pretty good (82 percent retention); best in a retirement plan

- Worst year over the past decade was 1990 (-13 percent) and best year over the past ten years was 1991 (+51 percent)

Medium Risk

Mairs and Power Growth
800-304-7404
• U.S. growth fund that does particularly well during bull markets

• Has outperformed 95 percent of its peers as well as 95 percent of all mutual funds

• Worst year over the past decade was 1987 (-2 percent) and best year was 1995 (+48 percent)

• Extremely low expense ratio and fantastic tax minimization (93 percent)

New Perspective
800-421-4120
• A global stock portfolio (U.S. and foreign stocks)

• Has outperformed 90 percent of its peers and has been safer than 95 percent of its global stock peers

• Worst year over the past decade was 1990 (-2 percent); best year was 1993 (+27 percent)

• Tax minimization is quite good (89 percent retention); expense control is exceptional

Oakmark
800-625-6275
• Growth stock portfolio that has outperformed 95 percent of its peers and all other funds

• Has been safer than half of its competitors. Worst year since inception was 1994 (+3 percent) and best year was 1992 (+40 percent); predictability of returns is very good

• Tax minimization (93 percent) has been fantastic; you will also like other funds in the family

Low-to-Medium Risk

Flag Investors Value Builder
800-767-3524
• Approximately two thirds of the portfolio is in common stocks; the balance is in bonds and cash

• Some of the highest returns possible for a balanced fund with higher-than-average risk

• Superb tax minimization; control over expenses has also been quite good

• Worst year since inception was 1994 (0 percent); best year was 1995, (+33 percent)

Greenspring
800-366-3863
• A balanced fund with roughly two thirds in stocks and one third in bonds and cash

• Management is considered great; tax savings have been quite good

• Has outperformed 90 percent of its peers and 75 percent of all mutual funds

• Worst year over the past decade was 1990 (-6 percent) and best year was 1996 (+23 percent)

SMART MONEY

To create a well-diversified portfolio, you only need to include one or two funds from just a few different categories. "High risk" can be satisfied by an aggressive growth or small-company growth fund. "Medium risk" can be accomplished with an equity-income or growth and income fund. "Low-to-medium risk" can be fulfilled with utilities and high-yield bond funds. And "low risk" is accomplished with a money market account.

T. Rowe Price Equity-Income
800-638-5660
• A growth & income fund (almost all U.S. stocks)

• Has been safer than 94 percent of all growth and income funds

• Over the past decade: Worst year was 1990 (-7 percent) and best year was 1995 (+33 percent)

• Recommended more for those who want to be in stocks; predictability of returns is high

Low Risk

MFS Utilities
800-637-2929
• One of the few equity portfolios that can be recommended for this risk level

• Has outperformed 95 percent of its peers and 80 percent of all mutual funds

• Since inception: Worst year was 1994 (-4 percent) and best year was 1995 (+33 percent)

• Management is rated as excellent; the best utilities fund around

MainStay High-Yield Corporate Bond
800-624-6782
• Total return and risk reduction for high-yield bond category are amazing

• Has been safer than 90 percent of its peers but has outperformed 95 percent of the group

- Current income is about as high as it gets; tax minimization is pretty good

- Over the past decade: Worst year was 1990 (-8 percent) and best year was 1991 (+32 percent)

Warburg Pincus Global Fixed Income
800-927-2874
- A global bond fund that has been safer than 75 percent of its peers

- The only fund in my book to receive a perfect score in all areas

- For a bond fund, tax minimization is good (64 percent); predictability of returns is very high

- Since inception: Worst year was 1994 (-5 percent) and best year was 1995 (+20 percent)

Before You Buy

Except for money market funds, you should not invest in any type of fund unless you have an understanding of the risks and rewards. Just because the stock market has been constantly hitting new highs or the bond market has had a substantial short-term loss does not mean that you should act. Instead, make your decisions based on an overall financial plan. Once you feel positive about a market and have researched a specific fund, you are ready to invest. If you want to be in the stock or bond market but are unsure which fund is best for you, strongly consider an index fund. (These index funds typically outperform at least two thirds of their peers.)

When to Sell a Fund

The majority of mutual fund investors are guilty of impatience. Investors now define "long term" as a year and will often switch from one fund to another after a disappointing quarter or year—particularly if they have read an article about the quarter's (or year's) hot performers. In most cases, this is a big mistake.

Remember why you went into the fund originally. Presumably one of those reasons was professional management. The fact that a fund underperforms over one or two years is not a good reason to sell. Such underperformance does not mean that management is no longer talented. It may mean that management has selected a group of securities that have, overall, been out of favor with the market for the period, but these out-of-favor securities could come roaring back next month, quarter or year.

If your fund has underperformed its peer group average for each of the last three years, the reason lies in one or more of the following: a high expense ratio; poor security selection; and risk reduction.

There are a number of "underperformers" whose risk profile is so attractive as to make the fund a recommended buy. Most investors are willing to give up some of the upside potential for a moderate or severe reduction in risk or volatility.

If you have given the fund a chance for a few years and it still has not been satisfactory, either on a return or risk-adjusted return basis, then you should sell it. Before selling, have an alternative in mind.

Investing in Annuities

An annuity is an investment you make with an insurance company, which represents a contractual relationship between you and the company. Although they're offered only by the insurance industry, annuities have little, if anything, in common with insurance coverage. Annuities are marketed and sold through brokerage firms, insurance agencies, banks, savings and loan institutions, financial planners, and investment advisers.

When you purchase, or invest, in an annuity, you are given certain assurances by the insurance company. These promises depend upon the company issuing the contract (the investment) and the type of annuity chosen. There are two main types of annuities, fixed-rate and variable.

• **Fixed-Rate Annuities**. These are very similar to bank CDs. You make a one-time investment (called a "single premium") and receive a guaranteed rate of return for the duration of the contract, anywhere from one to ten years. Generally, the longer the period of time, the greater the rate of interest.

• **Variable Annuities**. This kind of annuity is similar to a mutual fund family. You select from one or more different investment portfolios, called "sub-accounts." Usually you're offered a wide range of choices, from ultra-conservative (a money market account) to quite aggressive (Pacific Basin stocks). As with a mutual fund family, you can change the allocation of your money at any time, and you can add additional money to your investment (called a "flexible premium").

Four Parties to an Annuity

There are always four parties to each annuity:

- The insurer

- The contract owner

- The annuitant

- The beneficiary

Often, the contract owner and the annuitant are the same person.

The Insurer

The insurance company you choose, known as the insurer, invests your money according to what you specify on the application and the type of annuity offered. For a fixed-rate annuity, the only thing you have to choose is the duration of the contract (e.g., anywhere from one to ten years). For a variable annuity, the biggest decision is picking the subaccounts and allocating your portfolio among them (e.g., 50 percent in growth, 20 percent in high-yield bonds, 30 percent in global stocks). The insurance company then turns your money directly over to a professional management company that handles the actual investing.

In addition to placing the money, the insurer makes certain promises, covered in greater detail later in this chapter, which are contained within the annuity contract. Items such as adding more money, making withdrawals, cancellation penalties, and guarantees are all spelled out.

The Contract Owner

An annuity investor is technically known as the contract owner. A contract owner is similar to the purchaser (shareholder) of a mutual fund. Contract owners have the right and ability to add more money, terminate the agreement, withdraw part or all of the money, or change the parties named in the contract.

The Annuitant

The one party to an annuity that is difficult to understand is the annuitant. The best way to explain the annuitant is by analogy. When you purchase life insurance, an insured is named. Sometimes the insured is also the owner, but other times the owner is a third party (a company, a trust, a spouse, etc.). The policy is in force until the owner terminates the contract, fails to make any required premium payments, or the insured dies.

Similarly, an annuity remains in force until the contract owner makes a change or the annuitant dies. Thus, the annuitant is like the "insured" in a life insurance policy. The annuitant, like an insured, has no voice in or control of the contract. The annuitant does not have the power to make withdrawals or deposits, change the names of the parties to the agreement, or terminate the contract. And just as is the case when you purchase life insurance on someone else (the insured), the annuitant usually must sign the contract. The primary difference is that the death of the annuitant does not necessarily mean the contract is about to come to an end.

The person you name as the annuitant (the "insured") can be anyone: yourself, your spouse, parent, child, relative, friend, or neighbor. The only qualification is that the named annuitant is actually a person (i.e., not a living trust, corporation, partnership, etc.) currently living who is under a certain age. Most companies require that the annuitant be under the age of seventy-five when the contract is initially signed, but this varies by company.

Older Annuitants

There are some pluses and minuses to naming an older or terminal person as the annuitant. On the plus side, the guaranteed death benefit will kick in faster. Also, any and all penalties will disappear (since death is considered an involuntary event). On the minus side, once the annuitant reaches a certain age, typically somewhere between seventy and eighty, certain death benefits may be frozen. Additionally, the death of the annuitant could trigger taxes owed within five years unless the owner and annuitant are spouses.

The Beneficiary

Like a vice president of a country, the beneficiary is of little meaning until the death of a certain individual. In the case of an annuity, the beneficiary is "waiting" for the death of the annuitant. And, as with a life insurance policy, the beneficiary of an annuity has no voice in the control or management of the policy. The named beneficiary(s) can be a spouse, children, friends, relatives, neighbors, trusts, corporations, or partnerships. Additionally, multiple beneficiaries can be designated in varying proportions (i.e., 25 percent to Mary Jones, 15 percent to Jack Jones, 10 percent to Edward Smith, and 50 percent to the Nelson Family Trust).

How the Contract Is Driven

In the past, all annuity contracts were "annuitant driven," meaning that certain provisions or sections of the annuity contract came into being if the annuitant died, reached a certain age, or became disabled. Provisions such as a waiver of any insurance company penalty, the death benefit, IRS penalty, and/or the required annuitization or distribution of the contract became effective based on what happened to the annuitant.

Today a growing minority of annuity contracts are **owner driven,** meaning that the events described above (i.e., death, disability, or reaching a certain age) are based on whether or not something happens to the contract owner rather than to the annuitant. A few annuity contracts have a provision that some sections or provisions of the contract can come into play if either the owner, co-owner, and/or annuitant dies, reaches the age of annuitization, or becomes disabled. Such either/or substitutes make the annuity contract more flexible and usually more appealing.

Common Setups

In the case of a married couple, it is quite common for the contract owner to be one spouse and the annuitant to be the other. (A few companies allow co-ownership, in which case both spouses can be owners.) In the event of the untimely death of the annuitant, the assets would then go directly to the surviving spouse.

A single person, widow, or widower will usually name himself as the contract owner and annuitant, and a loved one or entity (e.g., a living trust, charity, corporation, etc.) as the beneficiary. By making such an election, the individual retains complete control and dominion over the investment during his or her lifetime. Upon the person's death, the money will automatically pass to the intended heir.

The contract owner can change the beneficiary or beneficiaries at any time at his or her discretion, without anyone else's consent. You do not need to notify someone that they have been listed as a beneficiary of your annuity, nor do you have to tell them that they have been removed as a beneficiary.

Why People Like Annuities

As indicated at the beginning of the chapter, fixed-rate and variable annuities are very different types of investment vehicles (a little later in this chapter, we'll look more at their distinctive features), but there are a few very important characteristics that all annuities share that make them attractive to particular kinds of investors.

Tax-Deferred Growth

One of the biggest advantages that sets annuities apart from other investments is that they allow your money to grow and compound tax-deferred. The only time taxes are due is upon the withdrawal of any growth (capital appreciation) or interest, and only upon the amount actually withdrawn (in contrast to, for example, a mutual fund, for which you must declare interest, dividends, and capital gains every year).

The deferral of taxes can make a huge difference in how your money grows over time. For example, an investment that grows 6 percent annually will double in value every twelve years. If you are paying 33 percent in income taxes, though, that same investment will take eighteen years to double since it is only growing at 4 percent (6 percent minus 2 percent for taxes). You and I only have so many doubling periods until we die or retire and each doubling period is substantial, as $100,000 grows to $200,000, and $200,000 grows to $400,000, and so on.

The growth-oriented investor can end up with an investment worth hundreds of thousands of dollars more simply by choosing an annuity.

In theory, the avoidance of income taxes can last well beyond your lifetime. When the contract owner dies, a surviving spouse named as the beneficiary can take over the investment and thus postpone any income tax. The contract would then continue until the death of the surviving spouse. If the remaining spouse later remarries and names the "new" spouse as the beneficiary, the tax deferral could last longer still.

Tax-Free Exchanges

For traditional mutual fund investors, transfers (also known as switches) within a mutual fund family or from one fund company to another results in a taxable event. Mutual fund groups also usually charge a $5 fee for each switch. With a variable annuity, on the other hand, you can reallocate your portfolio among subaccounts as often as you like (moving from one fund to another) without owing any tax. The typical variable annuity allows up to twelve switches per year at no charge. Annuities also allow you to move your money from one company to another without incurring taxes. This move is known as a "1035 exchange" and is named after the Internal Revenue Code (IRC) section that allows such exchanges. Please note that in order for you to take advantage of this, the money must go directly from one insurer to another.

Avoidance of Probate

Since you always name a beneficiary with an annuity, the value of the account is allowed to pass free of probate to the beneficiary. In other words, a trust and will are not necessary with this investment.

Probate is a messy, lengthy, and expensive process. It took over fifteen years to probate the

To Live and Die in L.A.

The chart below shows the statutory probate fees for the state of California. Some states have fees that are even greater. The fees are based on the gross value of your estate (you cannot deduct any liens or mortgages), not its net value.

Estate's gross value	Probate fee	Estate's gross value	Probate fee
$100,000	$6,300	$700,000	$30,300
$200,000	$10,300	$800,000	$34,300
$300,000	$14,300	$900,000	$38,300
$400,000	$18,300	$1,000,000	$42,300
$500,000	$22,300	$2,000,000	$62,300
$600,000	$26,300	$3,000,000	$82,300

estate of Howard Hughes; over ten years in the case of Marilyn Monroe. The lawyers who probated John Wayne's estate made so much money in the process that they closed down their firm once the Duke's estate was finally closed.

The amount you will spend on probate and executor (the person who settles your estate after you are gone) fees depends upon the gross value of your estate (e.g., the value of all of your assets, including boats, cars, stocks, bank accounts, and real estate, not reduced by any outstanding mortgages or debts). In California, an estate that has a gross value of $100,000 will pay court-ordered fees of $6,300 or more. Probate and executor fees increase as the size of your estate increases.

The Exclusion Ratio

Upon annuitization of a variable or fixed-rate contract, an exclusion ratio is determined by the insurer, using tables provided by the IRS. This ratio, or formula, determines the portion of each check that is considered a return of capital—and therefore not taxed—and the amount that is considered growth and/or interest, which is fully taxed.

The exclusion ratio varies depending upon the life expectancy of the annuitant, based on mortality tables, and the annuitization period selected by the contract owner. The longer the period, the smaller the ratio.

If relatively little growth or income has accumulated in the account, then most of each check will be a return of principal and therefore not taxable. Thus, annuitization over five years could result in an exclusion ratio of close to 85 percent (literally 85 percent of all distributions made would not be taxable). The same-size contract annuitized over eight years would have more time for accumulation on the undistributed balance and would therefore have a smaller exclusion ratio.

Annuitization

Most annuity contracts allow annuitization, which permits you to pay out both the principal and interest (or growth) in your account over a period of time—anywhere from a few years to the remainder of your life. The advantage of annuitization over other forms of liquidation or withdrawal is that disbursements are tax-favored, in that portion of the withdrawals that is a return of your original investment, or principal, is not taxed. With systematic withdrawal plans, or occasional withdrawals, there is no tax-favored treatment. When a contract is annuitized, the contract owner decides whether to receive checks on a monthly, quarterly, semiannual, or annual basis. The disadvantage of annuitization is that, in general, once started the process cannot be altered.

Why People Think Twice about Annuities

Just as annuities offer special benefits, they also carry some restrictions and expenses you should be aware of before you rush out and invest all of your money in one. The disadvantages of annuities are:

1. A potential IRS penalty

2. A potential insurance company penalty

3. No special tax treatment

IRS Penalty

Since annuities are tax-advantaged (they offer tax-deferred growth), they also carry a penalty for early withdrawal, just like an IRA. If you withdraw any growth or income (rather than principal) from an annuity prior to age fifty-nine and a half, you also have to pay the IRS a 10 percent penalty. If you die, of course, the IRS waives all penalties. Additionally, if the annuitant becomes disabled as defined in Section 72 of the Internal Revenue Code, the penalty is also waived.

Annuitization will also enable you to avoid any penalty, but annuitization must be elected by the contract owner within one year of investing in the annuity (the age of the owner is irrelevant).

Insurance Company Penalty

In most cases, the insurance company will also impose a penalty, also called a surrender charge, if you withdraw your money soon after establishing your annuity. Each company has its own penalty schedule, and you and your adviser should look at this closely when shopping for an annuity. The penalty period could last for ten or more years, and the penalty itself could be as high as 10 percent for the entire ten-year period. Fortunately, most companies have a penalty period of only five to eight years, the penalty typically starts off at 7 percent, and the penalty itself usually declines each year.

Most annuities do allow you to withdraw up to 10 percent of your principal (the money you invested in the annuity, rather than the growth and income earned by it) per year without cost, fee, or penalty. Some companies calculate the free withdrawal based upon the greater of current value or principal contribution(s).

For example, an annuity may state that its penalty lasts for six years and is structured as "6-5-4-3-2-1-0 thereafter." This means that "excess" withdrawals (those greater than 10 percent of the principal) made during the first six years are subject to a penalty, and the penalty decreases each year. A withdrawal made during the first year would be subject to a 6 percent penalty; money taken out during the second year would be penalized 5 percent, and so on.

A few companies allow free withdrawals of up to 15 percent per year. Still other companies allow free withdrawals of growth at any time of 10 to 15 percent that is based on the current value of the contract (which would be principal plus growth). Whatever rate your company allows, keep in mind two points:

• Close to 75 percent of all people who invest in an annuity never take any money out.

• The restriction on withdrawals eventually disappears.

No Special Tax Treatment

Unlike most investment assets held for at least eighteen months, annuities do not qualify for capital gains treatment. Taxable withdrawals are all taxed as ordinary income, with the top federal rate being 39.6 percent. (The maximum long-term capital gains rate is 20 percent.)

As a result, as compared to a tax–efficient mutual fund (such as Vanguard's S&P 500 Index Fund, which has an historical tax efficiency of somewhere between 91 and 94 percent), the tax rate on the annuity is about twice as high as what the mutual fund investor will eventually pay when a liquidation takes place.

Additionally, there is the issue of death. When someone inherits an annuity, there is no "step-up in basis." A step-up in basis means that the heir receives the asset as if he or she had just bought it on the day of your death (for example, you may have bought it for $10,000 and on your date of death it may be worth $75,000; your heir now has a cost basis of $75,000). Any sale by the heir will be treated, for tax purposes, as if the heir had paid $75,000 (the new cost basis). In other words, if the heir sells it for $76,000, there will be a long-term capital gain of $1,000.

Most assets, including stocks, mutual funds, and real-estate holdings, do get a step-up in basis; this is not the case with fixed-rate or variable annuities. So in the example above, when an heir liquidates an annuity that has grown from $10,000 to $75,000, ordinary income taxes will be due on the full $65,000 gain.

Fixed-Rate versus Variable

We've covered the general characteristics, both positive and negative, that apply equally to both fixed-rate and variable annuities. Now let's look at features that are particular to each type of annuity.

Low-Load Sources

If you are interested in no-load or low-load variable annuities, consider the following companies:

Jack White Value Advantage Plus
Total expenses: 0.46%
Surrender charge: none
800-622-3699

Vanguard Variable Annuity Plan
Total expenses: 0.61%
Surrender charge: none
800-523-9954

Providian Life The Adviser's Edge
Total expenses: 0.66%
Surrender charge: none
800-866-6007

Northwestern Mutual Select, Acct. B
Total expenses: 0.70
Surrender charge: none
414-299-1515

Pacific Life Pacific Portfolios
Total expenses: 0.83%
Surrender charge: lasts for seven years
800-722-2333

Schwab Variable Annuity
Total expenses: 0.86%
Surrender charge: none
800-838-0650

Principal Premier Variable
Total expenses: 0.91%
Surrender charge: none
800-247-4123

Best of America American Future Annuity
Total expenses: 0.95%
Surrender charge: lasts seven years
800-848-6331

John Hancock MarketPlace
Total expenses: 1.00%
Surrender charge: none
888-742-6262

Fidelity Retirement Reserves
Total expenses: 1.08%
Surrender charge: lasts five years
800-544-2442

Why People Choose Fixed-Rate Annuities

Fixed-rate annuities attract conservative investors. For people who ordinarily invest in CDs and money market funds, annuities usually offer the same safety, but often a higher rate of return. This

Commissions

Most insurance companies pay a commission for every annuity contract sale, though they do not charge you for this commission. When you buy a mutual fund (with the exception of no-load funds), the commission is usually taken out of your investment, producing an immediate decrease in your investment capital. With a variable annuity, on the other hand, 100 percent of your investment goes to work immediately.

Nonetheless, the broker or adviser you deal with does gets paid a commission from the insurance company. A commission is allocated for and paid regardless of whether or not you use a stockbroker, insurance agent, or financial planner. If you deal directly with the insurance company, they will either keep the commission or pay it out to one of their producers. So it is always in your best interest to make sure that the fee goes to someone who is working on your behalf, and who will be available to answer any questions or facilitate any changes you might have now or in the future.

is because the insurance industry knows that most people keep money in an annuity indefinitely. They can therefore commit funds to longer-maturing, higher-yielding bonds and mortgages and pass along some of that increased yield to you. Fixed-rate annuities do offer less liquidity than money market funds, however, though you can always make partial withdrawals. Or you can set up your annuity to provide you with regular income.

In fact, customers who are interested in such regular income often choose fixed-rate annuities over other types of traditionally safe investments. The income comes either from annuitization (discussed earlier on page 119) or through a systematic withdrawal program (SWP). A systematic withdrawal plan is a way of getting monthly checks and also reducing your risk. It's really a type of dollar-cost averaging *in reverse*, in that the same amount of money is withdrawn from your account on a regular basis. Just as dollar-cost averaging mitigates the effect of natural market fluctuations on your investing, systematic withdrawal balances your withdrawals. Either way, the yield or monthly return is often higher than it is with other alternatives such as CDs, money market accounts, or certain government obligations.

Safety

Conservative investors also like the unusual safety of fixed-rate annuities, in which the principal is guaranteed at all times, regardless of the amount. There are very few investments that can make this claim. In fact, the only others are accounts of up to $100,000 at financial institutions insured by the FDIC or FSLIC and certain types of life insurance contracts. Interest from U.S. Government securities is guaranteed, but the face value of such securities is only guaranteed if the securities are held until maturity.

Of course, this guarantee is only as solid as the company making it. Even though annuities have close to a perfect track record, some insurance companies are safer than others. Fortunately, there are a number of highly respected, unbiased companies that rate insurance companies as to their current financial soundness and ability to pay future claims.

The best known annuity-rating service is A. M. Best, an Oldwick, New Jersey, company that has been in the business since 1899. The highest rating an insurance company can receive is A++ (superior); the second–highest rating is A+ (superior). The lowest rating is F (in liquidation).

SMART SOURCES

Here are some companies with an A++ or A+ rating:

USG
800-369-3690
A+

Lincoln Benefit Life
800-395-9888
A+

Penn Mutual
800-818-8184
A+

SafeCo
800-280-9002
A+

First Colony
888-325-5433
A++

Unlike high-yield bonds, which provide a higher return as a trade-off for increased risk, you usually get very little, if any, extra return by buying a fixed-rate annuity from a lesser-rated company. Therefore, most investors should limit themselves to companies that have an A++ or A+ rating, of which there are several dozen to choose from.

Savvy insurance advisers will only recommend annuities and insurance products to their clients if the insurer has a top rating from both A. M. Best and any one of the other leading rating companies, Moody's, Standard & Poor's, or Duff and Phelps.

Variable Annuities: Special Benefits and Costs

There are a couple of both positive and negative features that apply specifically to variable annuities, which distinguish them from a mutual fund. On the one hand, variable annuities provide a guaranteed death benefit, which can provide security and peace of mind to investors concerned about preserving their retirement money. On the other hand, there is also a cost associated with this benefit.

Guaranteed Death Benefit

A variable annuity almost always contains a guaranteed death benefit. The guarantee insures that the beneficiary will receive the greater of all investments (principal contributed by the owner) minus any withdrawals or the value of the account as of the annuitant's date of death. This makes the variable annuity an ideal investment for an older couple who want a high income stream or growth to offset inflation. You can name yourself as the annuitant and invest aggressively to maximize income or growth, and at the same time remain secure knowing that upon your death, your spouse is guaranteed to inherit, at a minimum, whatever principal you've invested minus any withdrawals along the way. There is no investment, outside of the insurance industry, that provides such protection.

The death benefit charge, also called a mortality and expense fee, ranges from 0 percent (Lincoln National Director, 800-248-0838, and Schwab Variable Annuity, 800-838-0650) to 2.72 percent (Aetna Variable Annuity Account D, MAP V Highest—qualified money only, 800-232-5422) annually, depending upon the insurer and terms of the variable annuity contract. The most common mortality charge is 1.25 percent. Whatever the fee charged by your particular insurer, it can never be increased; the fact that the fee is "frozen" is clearly spelled out in every variable annuity contract, and the exact amount of the fee is described in the prospectus. This is a hidden fee, though, in that it will not be shown on any of your quarterly or annual statements. Rather, it is deducted every year from your total return, just as mutual fund companies deduct their expenses.

Several annuities even offer an "enhanced death benefit." Most commonly this means that the minimum death benefit is "stepped-up" to the principal plus interest on that principal compounded at 5 percent per year, up to a cap of 200 percent of the principal. This compounding also typically stops once the owner (or annuitant in some contracts) reaches a specific age, usually 75. This means that not only is your principal guaranteed, but you are also assured of a minimum return

How Expensive Are the Expenses?

Setting aside any potential surrender charge, the two main charges associated with a variable annuity are the *fund expense* (the fee paid to the mutual fund or management company overseeing the investment portfolios) and the *mortality and expense risk* (the guaranteed death benefit). The table below shows the average fund expense and total expense for the most popular investment categories within a variable annuity. (The figures are as of the middle of 1998.)

Portfolio type (subaccount)	Average fund expense (%)	Average total expense (%)
Aggressive growth	0.95	2.21
Balanced	0.84	2.12
Corporate bond	0.69	1.94
Government bond	0.64	1.90
Growth	0.86	2.12
Growth & income	0.67	1.94
High-yield bond	0.80	2.09
International bond	1.12	2.42
International stock	1.15	2.42
Money market	0.52	1.79
Specialty (sector)	1.05	2.34
Equity average	**0.82**	**2.09**
Fixed-income average	**0.74**	**2.00**

of 5 percent a year until your money has doubled.

Additionally, variable annuities levy a very modest contract maintenance charge, commonly $35 per year, though it can range from $0 to $120 depending upon the company. Several companies do not impose this charge if the value of the account is above a certain level.

Why People Choose Variable Annuities

Variable annuities combine the flexibility, features, and high-growth potential of a strong mutual fund family with tax-deferred growth and an extra measure of safety.

Unlike mutual funds, variable annuities allow you to make exchanges among the different sub-accounts or make a 1035 exchange and move your money from one company to another without any income tax consequences.

The death benefit that most variable contracts provide (or "enhanced death benefit" with some insurers), is a real plus psychologically with older investors. Even though this benefit is rarely claimed, it gives some investors the safety that enables them to invest more heavily in equities.

Perhaps the best candidate for a variable annuity is an individual or couple in a high tax bracket who want to enjoy tax-deferred growth for a number of years and then structure their contract so that they receive monthly income. Tax deferral means a greater growth rate, which means that any periodic income stream will be higher than with a taxable investment, since there is more principal to tap.

Variable annuities are also well-suited for people who want a flexible retirement savings vehicle but either do not qualify for an IRA or want to put away more than the allowed $2,000 per year. Also, while IRAs (with the exception of Roth IRAs) require you to begin withdrawing money after reaching age seventy and a half, variable annuities do not have this restriction.

Inside a Retirement Plan

During 1996 and 1997, close to half of variable annuity sales were done inside an IRA or other qualified retirement plan. Since IRA and retirement accounts grow and compound tax-deferred, just like annuities, an annuity inside a retirement plan provides no additional tax benefit. As a general rule, the expenses associated with an annuity are about 1 percent higher per year than they are in a similar-type mutual fund. The question, then, becomes whether or not there is any benefit to investing in an annuity within a retirement plan.

The only special advantage an annuity provides in this situation is the guaranteed death benefit, and it comes at a high cost. It has been estimated that less than one half of 1 percent of variable annuity contracts are surrendered each year due to death or disability, but the charge for this feature generally ranges from 0.75 to 1.25 percent annually. Thus, the odds of someone benefiting from a guaranteed death benefit are extremely slim.

Buying Real Estate and REITs

THE KEYS

• Investing in land and buildings has an emotional appeal and many potential financial advantages. But investing directly in real estate requires considerable time and effort.

• It's vitally important to determine property values accurately before you buy.

• Investing in real estate investment trusts (REITs) is far simpler—and for most investors, more sensible—than purchasing properties outright.

By providing us with places to live, eat, shop, work, and play, real estate touches all of our lives. Its value in part lies in our attachment to or dependence upon land, residences, shopping centers, office complexes, recreational centers, warehouses, and public buildings.

The hold that land and the buildings on it has on us can be both deep and powerful. Consider the famous ending to the film *Gone With the Wind*: Scarlett O'Hara didn't console herself over the loss of Rhett Butler by thinking of how best to position her interests in railroads, newspapers, or gold mining operations. She thought about land—the red earth of Tara—and suddenly she was able to face the next day.

We can touch land, walk around on it, dream about what it means to us, look at the buildings on it, imagine other buildings that could be on it. As a result, we may tend to think of land and residences and commercial properties as being somehow more real than many other investments. Still, the question remains: Is real estate a worthwhile investment?

Is Real Estate Right for You?

Should you invest in real estate? Many investors are tempted to answer yes almost immediately. For starters, real estate is treated favorably under the income tax laws:

• Interest on mortgage payments can be deducted, as can property taxes and other "use" fees.

• Buildings and structures (but not land itself) can be depreciated—which means the cost of the building can be deducted in small increments over a long period of time.

• Improvements to income-generating property, such as fixtures and appointments (e.g., carpeting, drapes, furniture, paintings, etc.) can be either written off in the year of acquisition as expenses or depreciated over a short period of time.

All of these investor-friendly tax benefits can shelter income from the property or other taxable income.

Furthermore, our monetary system is often inclined to lend money collateralized by real estate sometimes at rates below inflation, so leverage can be achieved relatively inexpensively. In other words, you can purchase a valuable property by paying only 10 percent of the price as your down payment—that's the leverage. As an example, let's take a $10 million office building that has a $9 million mortgage with a 6 percent, 30-year, fixed-rate mortgage that is appreciating (through a combination of inflation and/or an increase in rents) at 10 percent per year. This scenario would yield solid profits. You've invested only $1 million (the other $9 million has been borrowed), yet the entire $10 million is appreciating at 10 percent annually— that's essentially double what you've invested. Once you account for the true, after-tax cost of the borrowed money (6 percent interest deducted from your taxes results in a "real" cost of 3 percent for someone who pays 50 percent of his income in taxes), which would be $270,000 (3 percent of a $9 million mortgage) produces a net gain using just these figures of $730,000 per year. (The $1 million appreciation, which isn't taxed until the building is sold, minus $270,000, which is the after-tax cost of the borrowed money).

The Upside

Beyond such issues as taxes, leverage, and inflation, however, there is an even more basic reason for real estate's seemingly universal appeal. Real estate is a limited resource that meets a fundamental human need. Its value is determined by supply and demand. No human being can manufacture any more land. It's not surprising, then, that despite ups and downs in local markets, real estate continues, as a general rule, to rise in value over time. In part, this has to do with such forces as government regulation, environmentalism, and general inflation, each of which can help to drive up the cost of labor, materials, and land to build on.

Certainly, those who invest in income-producing real estate, such as domestic rental properties, can benefit in a number of different ways. For instance, income-producing real estate will eventually, if not immediately, provide cash distribution from property operations. These cash distributions should increase over time. In addition, income-producing real estate, as noted above, enjoys many tax benefits. What's more, appreciation of real estate is normally taxed at the lower capital gains rates.

Then there's the buildup of equity. Each mortgage payment comprises interest and principal. Every time a payment is made, the debt is reduced a little bit and the equity is increased. And with many income-producing properties, the owner is simply paying off a loan with rent dollars supplied by the tenant.

Finally, there's the possibility of significant appreciation. Improvements to the property can lead to higher rents, and add to the value of the property—and therefore its resale price. With market changes and inflation, the property can appreciate significantly.

The Downside

Those are the possible pluses. Now take a look at the dramatic—and for most investors, potentially overwhelming—pitfalls: Managing income-producing real estate properties is usually a full-time job. You are dealing with tenants, maintenance people, city regulators, tax collectors, and detailed bookkeeping. Developing an effective set of strategies for buying and selling properties at a profit also requires considerable devotion. Even then, you will be subject to a bewildering array of market forces (stock market performance, interest rates, social trends, neighborhood demographics), few of which will be easy to understand, much less control. And you'll need to know how to determine when to sell a property and for what price or terms.

Is My Home an Investment?

First, most of us are best advised to keep in mind that a home is a long-term investment; in fact, the

National Association of Realtors notes that it takes five years to break even on a home (due to commissions, closing costs, and repairs). If you buy a home, do so because you want to live there, because you can afford to do so, and because making that purchase improves your overall quality of life.

Don't buy a home expecting to sell it at a significant profit three or four years later. There are too many variables at work, and too many opportunities for heartache and serious financial setback, to mix together investing in real estate and owning a place to live.

With those warnings in place, the following (basic) advice on evaluating real estate investments is offered for those who, on careful reflection, decide that this complex and difficult area of investment is worth pursuing.

Finding Out What It's Worth

The two most commonly used methods to determine the value of an income-producing property are the market data approach and the gross multiplier approach. Is a property worth what a seller says it's worth? That's the question at the heart of most real estate investing.

The Market Data Approach

To determine basic property values, the market data analysis approach looks at prices paid for similar properties. Basically, you need to locate comparable properties—or "comps"—that have sold recently. (The key word here is "recently.") A comp would be in the same neighborhood, have similar units (e.g., two bedrooms and two baths) and amenities (e.g. pool, tennis courts), and be the same age. By comparing your property with several comps, you can draw a conclusion as to its relative value. If you're new to real estate, you'll probably want to work with a qualified appraiser a few times before you start developing these figures on your own.

The Gross Multiplier Approach

To analyze the overall value of a property in order to determine how much revenue the property will generate for you, the process is more complex. The simplest method in this situation is the gross multiplier approach. (There's a more sophisticated technique called the capitalization rate approach, but it's really not for newcomers. You may want to ask a qualified appraiser or other real estate professional to run this kind of analysis for you.)

Because it focuses on the property's rental income, this method ignores differences between properties in vacancies, operating expenses, utilities, property taxes, and other such categories—as well as various financing issues and possible tax consequences. But in the final analysis, the capacity to produce income is much of what determines a property's value.

First, calculate your property's anticipated annual income. Then multiply the anticipated annual income by the gross multiplier factor. This gives you the total property value. As with the market data approach, apply the same calculations to recent comps and compare them with your property.

In most marketplaces, properties tend to reflect a factor of between five and nine times their annual gross rents. When tenants are responsible for their own utilities, the gross multiplier factor tends to be a little higher. Even so, a factor of between six and seven and a half is fairly common, and that represents a good basic yardstick. Thus, a property generating $100,000 in annual gross rents would bring between $600,000 and $750,000.

What You Should Earn

Let's assume you're interested in purchasing an income-producing property. Before you invest, as a good rule of thumb compare its return to that of a high-yield bond. If the property won't do at least as well, buy the high-yield bond fund instead.

As an example, let's assume that barely rated junk bonds (those rated BB or B) are yielding 8 percent. If the purchase price of the rental property is $100,000, you should come away with $8,000 in rent after paying for any management, bookkeeping, maintenance, property taxes (after adjusting for their deductibility), and loan payments (the after-tax cost).

Many real estate authorities would challenge this advice, pointing to real estate's appreciation potential. But high-yield bonds are much more marketable than real estate, and the entry and exit fees are considerably lower—there's little or no cost to buy or sell high-yield bonds, compared to 6 to 7 percent in commissions and closing costs in the typical real estate deal. Plus, there is no "hassle factor" in owning high-yield bonds. They don't have tenants, need a fresh coat of paint, require the service of plumbers, entail constant calls to property managers, or send out late rent checks. And while the appreciation potential is more limited, so is the risk: a leveraged real estate investment can wipe out your entire investment.

Finally, bear in mind this last tip. Most successful real estate investors maintain that profits are made when they *buy* property, not when they sell it. By researching the market, analyzing the cash flow of a property, and securing the best financing, the knowledgeable investor can decrease risk and increase potential gain.

Real Estate Investment Vehicles

As noted, most investors simply aren't cut out for the work required to purchase and manage an individual income-producing real estate property. But that doesn't mean that you can't invest in real estate.

One increasingly popular investment vehicle is the Real Estate Investment Trust (REIT). A REIT is a business trust managed by trustees, somewhat like a mutual fund, that invests in mortgages and/or properties rather than stocks or bonds. According to the National Association of Real Estate Investment Trusts (NAREIT), REITs have on average outperformed both bonds and directly owned property since 1976. This industry group also points out that equity REITs (those that invest in property) have returned an average of 16 percent annually over the same period, nearly matching the S&P 500's gain of 16.6 percent (and in five of the last eight years, they have actually beaten the S&P 500, which is quite a feat when you consider how hot the stock market has been). Here is a table of comparative returns from NAREIT.

Period	Comparative Equity REITs (%)	Returns S&P 500 (%)
1 year (1996)	35.3	23.0
3 years (1994–96)	17.2	19.6
5 years (1992–96)	16.6	15.2
10 years (1987–96)	9.0	15.3
15 years (1982–96)	12.2	16.8
20 years (1977–96)	13.2	14.6

How They Work

The major differences between a real estate investment trust (REIT) and a public company such as IBM or GM is taxation and operating restrictions. Though most REITs are set up as corporations, they are not taxed as corporations. In REITs, as in mutual funds, profits are distributed to shareholders, who then report such distributions as taxable income.

REITs can be either public or private entities. Public REITs are traded on a stock exchange, similar to any other stock. First introduced in 1960, REITs have become extremely popular over the past few years. Just since the beginning of the decade, assets in REITs have grown from approximately $9 billion to over $200 billion.

• An **equity REIT** owns property—typically, several properties, though some own a single parcel of land or a partial interest in multiple properties. Most specialize in a particular type of property, such as shopping centers or medical buildings, or in a particular region of the country.

• A **mortgage REIT** simply lends money to real estate investors, using the property (and perhaps other assets of the borrower) as collateral. These are safer than equity REITs, but their potential for appreciation is more limited.

• In essence, equity REITs are similar to other equity investments, such as stocks, and mortgage REITs are more akin to buying debt instruments like bonds. There are also **hybrid REITs**, which are similar to a balanced mutual fund that invests in both stocks and bonds. A hybrid REIT owns property and mortgages. Hybrids provide the stability of a predictable income little influenced by real estate prices but also have the potential of appreciation by the sale or refinancing of properties that have gone up in value. They have more growth (or loss) potential than mortgage REITs, but in turn generate less current income. And they provide more current income than equity REITs, but offer less upside potential.

The table below shows the annual returns for the three different categories of REITs.

Year	Equity (%)	Mortgage (%)	Hybrid (%)
1997	20.3	3.8	10.8
1996	35.3	50.9	29.4
1995	15.3	63.4	23.0
1994	3.2	-24.3	4.0
1993	19.7	14.5	21.2
1992	14.6	1.9	16.6
1991	35.7	31.8	39.2
1990	-15.4	-18.4	-28.2
1989	8.8	-16.0	-12.1
1988	13.5	7.3	6.6
1987	-3.6	-15.7	-17.6
1986	19.2	19.2	18.8
1985	19.1	-5.2	4.3
1984	20.9	7.3	17.2
1983	30.6	16.9	29.9

If you're interested in investing in a vehicle that allows you to participate in the growth of the real estate industry, enjoy full liquidity, and spend no time dealing with the myriad logistical and maintenance issues traditionally related to property investment, REITs, or mutual funds that trade in REITs, are probably the way to go. For most investors, these stocks represent a realistic opportunity for hassle-free growth—although, because of the dividend payments, they carry certain tax implications you'll want to review with your tax specialist.

Should REITs Be Part of Your Portfolio?

REITs have a number of positive attributes. First, the typical REIT has a dividend yield comparable to fixed-income instruments such as bank CDs, government securities, money market funds, and high-quality corporate bonds. Unlike these traditional debt instruments, most REITs have a strong potential for appreciation. Values can be increased in several ways: lower interest rates, increased rents and occupancies, and a greater demand for real estate. However, even within each of the three categories described above, there can and has been a huge variation in performance.

The most conservative and safest types of property are (from least conservative to most): commercial net lease, regional malls, industrial properties, manufactured housing, and multifamily residential (apartments). High-risk properties, from least risky to most, are office buildings, shopping centers, self-storage centers, hotels and motels, and raw land. Raw land is the riskiest because it is not generating any cash flow, there are no structures to depreciate (meaning there is no shelter), plus there are costs to the owner for maintaining the property (e.g., property taxes, shrubbery removal, permits to build, engineering as well as contractor and architectural fees).

REIT Mutual Funds

As an alternative to selecting REITs on your own, there are mutual funds that specialize in REITs, with assets of close to $10 billion. Here are some of the best-known names in the industry.

Alliance Real Estate Investment Fund
P.O. Box 1520
Secaucus, NJ 07096
800-221-5672

CGM Realty Fund
1 International Pl.
Boston, MA 02110
800-345-4048

Cohen & Steers Realty Income Fund
757 3rd Ave.
N.Y., NY 10017
800-437-9912

Crabe Huson Real Estate Investment Fund
121 Southwest Morrison, Suite 1400
Portland, OR 97204
800-541-9732

Delaware REIT Portfolio Fund
1 Commerce Sq.
Philadelphia, PA 19103
800-231-8002

Fidelity Real Estate Securities Fund
P.O. Box 193
Boston, MA 02101
800-544-8888

Franklin Real Estate
777 Mariners Island Blvd.
San Mateo, CA 94404
800-342-5236

Morgan Stanley Real Estate Fund
1221 Ave. of the Americas, 21st Floor
N.Y., NY 10020
800-548-7786

Phoenix Real Estate Securities Fund
100 Bright Meadow Blvd.
Enfield, CT 06082
800-243-4361

Pioneer Real Estate Group
P.O. Box 9017
Boston, MA 02205
800-225-6292

Vanguard REIT Index Portfolio
P.O. Box 2600
Valley Forge, PA 19482
800-662-7447

Features You Should Look for in an Equity REIT

Before investing in an individual equity REIT, try to find ones that have several of the following characteristics:

1. All operations are administered by the REIT.

2. All properties owned are managed by the REIT.

3. There's full-integration—all purchases, sales, management, and construction are done by the REIT.

4. The assets are high quality.

5. There's a geographical focus (more important for small and mid-sized REITs).

6. It has a successful track record (the industry tends to be cyclical; look for management that has been through the good and the bad).

7. There's large insider ownership (it's a good sign if management has a sizable stake).

8. It has little or no debt (the marketplace is cautious about leverage).

You could also focus on REITs that are located in your area. That way you can evaluate the properties yourself and talk to management. You will also have a better feel for the economic climate.

Individual REITS to Contact

Listed below are examples of REITs that have a track record of at least three years.

Low Risk

Mortgage REITs

These represent about 5 percent of the REIT industry, and invest in individual mortgages, pools of mortgages, and government or agency-issued mortgage securities.

CWM Mortgage Holdings, Inc.
35 North Lake Ave.
Pasadena, CA 91101
800-669-2300
www.inmc.com
Trades on the NYSE: symbol CWM

Year	Change in Price per Share (%)	Yield (%)	Total Annual Return (%)
1996	26.5	9.2	35.7
1995	97.0	13.6	110.6
1994	-15.9	10.4	-5.5
1993	86.1	8.9	95.0
1992	-12.2	7.8	-4.4

Capstead Mortgage Corp.
2711 N. Haskell Ave., Suite 900
Dallas, TX 75204
800-358-2323
www.capstead.com
Trades on the NYSE: symbol CMO

Year	Change in Price per Share (%)	Yield (%)	Total Annual Return (%)
1996	57.4	13.8	71.2
1995	104.8	14.7	119.5
1994	-58.8	7.8	-51.0
1993	4.5	9.3	13.8
1992	33.6	11.1	44.7

Low-to-Moderate Risk

Commercial Net Leases

In the small office buildings, restaurants, and retail stores making up this group, the tenant manages the property and pays all the expenses, including property taxes, maintenance, insurance and utilities

Commercial Net Lease Realty, Inc.
400 E. South St., Suite 500
Orlando, FL 32801
407-422-1574
www.nnnreit.com
Trades on the NYSE: symbol NNN

SMART SOURCES

Aside from the traditional investment newspapers and magazines, you can find excellent coverage of REITs and real estate on a national level in *Real Estate Review*, a quarterly publication by Warren Gorham Lamont (212-971-5120), and *Emerging Trends in Real Estate*, published by the Real Estate Research Corporation (312-346-5885) and Equitable Real Estate Investment Management.

The three best sources for evaluating individual REITs are Value Line, Standard & Poor's, and NAREIT. Value Line provides the most analytical reports, but it covers fewer than twenty of the most popular REITs. Standard & Poor's has the most comprehensive coverage of REIT stocks.

What Matters

• Deciding between equity or mortgage REITs.

• Your risk level and the type of REIT.

• Quality management and property categories that make sense in the future.

• Highly capitalized REITs with long-term track records.

What Doesn't

• Total return, including changes in price per share, not just current yield.

• The commission involved in buying or selling REIT shares.

• The poor history of REITs in the 1970s and early 1980s.

Year	Change in Price per Share (%)	Yield (%)	Total Annual Return (%)
1996	24.5	9.3	33.8
1995	4.1	9.5	13.6
1994	-10.9	8.3	-2.6
1993	13.4	9.1	22.5
1992	24.4	11.1	35.5

TriNet Corporate Realty Trust, Inc.
4 Embarcadero Center, Suite 3150
San Francisco, CA 94111
415-391-4300
www.tricorp.com
Trades on the NYSE: symbol TRI

Year	Change in Price per Share (%)	Yield (%)	Total Annual Return (%)
1996	30.3	9.1	39.4
1995	-6.8	8.4	1.6
1994	5.9	8.6	14.5

Industrial Properties

Historically these warehouses, light industrial buildings, and business service buildings have very low vacancy rates and are usually occupied by a single tenant. There is less management required, and lower physical depreciation and capital expenditures.

CenterPoint Properties

401 N. Michigan Ave., 30th Floor
Chicago, IL 60611
312-346-5600
Trades on the NYSE: symbol CNT

Year	Change in Price per Share (%)	Yield (%)	Total Annual Return (%)
1996	41.6	7.0	48.6
1995	18.6	8.0	26.6
1994	-6.1	8.2	14.3

Bedford Property Investors, Inc.

270 Lafayette Circle
Lafayette, CA 94549
510-283-8910
Trades on the NYSE: symbol BED

Year	Change in Price per Share (%)	Yield (%)	Total Annual Return (%)
1996	22.8	7.0	29.8
1995	30.0	7.5	37.5
1994	12.8	7.3	20.1
1993	56.0	5.8	61.8
1992	25.0	0.0	25.0

Multifamily Units (Apartments)

These REITs try to become a dominate player in the area. Tenant turnover is the most difficult problem, and management is critical. Cash flow and expenses are fairly predictable.

BRE Properties, Inc.
1 Montgomery St., Suite 2500
San Francisco, CA 94104-5525
415-445-6530
www.breproperties.com
Trades on the NYSE: symbol BRE

Year	Change in Price per Share (%)	Yield (%)	Total Annual Return (%)
1996	38.9	7.4	46.3
1995	15.4	8.2	23.6
1994	-8.2	7.1	-1.1
1993	3.9	7.4	11.3
1992	14.1	8.5	22.6

United Dominion Realty Trust
10 South 6th St., Suite 203
Richmond, VA 23219-3802
804-780-2691
Trades on the NYSE: symbol UDR

Year	Change in Price per Share (%)	Yield (%)	Total Annual Return (%)
1996	3.3	6.4	9.7
1995	4.3	6.3	10.6
1994	0.9	5.5	6.4
1993	12.8	5.5	18.3
1992	22.4	6.4	28.8

Moderate-to-High Risk

Office Buildings

These suffered the greatest losses due to the over-building of the 1980s. Tenants have become much more selective in their choice of space, and leases tend to run 3 to 5 years.

CarrAmerica Realty Corp.
1700 Pennsylvania St., N.W.
Washington, DC 20006
202-624-7500
www.carramerica.com
Trades on the NYSE: symbol CRE

Year	Change in Price per Share (%)	Yield (%)	Total Annual Return (%)
1996	20.0	7.2	27.2
1995	35.4	9.7	45.1
1994	-21.7	7.6	14.1

Koger Equity, Inc.
3986 Blvd. Center Dr., Suite 101
Jacksonville, FL 32207
904-398-3403
www.koger.com
Trades on the NYSE: symbol KE

Year	Change in Price per Share (%)	Yield (%)	Total Annual Return (%)
1996	76.5	0.5	77.0
1995	46.6	0.0	46.6
1994	-14.7	0.0	-14.7
1993	83.8	0.0	83.8
1992	15.6	0.0	15.6

Shopping Centers

Construction is often rampant during good times, but when the economy slows, there may be insufficient business. Competition for consumers and with other centers nearby is high and one-stop shopping for convenience has become increasingly important.

Bradley Real Estate, Inc.
40 Skokie Blvd., Suite 600
Northbrook, IL 60062
847-272-9800
Trades on the NYSE: symbol BTR

Year	Change in Price per Share (%)	Yield (%)	Total Annual Return (%)
1996	33.3	9.8	43.1
1995	-11.5	8.7	-2.8
1994	-17.6	7.0	-10.6
1993	17.5	7.8	25.3
1992	26.0	9.6	35.6

Price REIT, Inc.
7979 Invanhoe Ave., Suite 524
La Jolla, CA 92037
619-551-2320
www.pricereit.com
Trades on the NYSE: symbol RET

Year	Change in Price per Share (%)	Yield (%)	Total Annual Return (%)
1996	76.5	10.1	48.8
1995	46.6	8.6	-1.9
1994	-14.7	8.6	14.6
1993	83.8	8.2	12.5
1992	15.6	8.3	14.7

Hotels and Motels

Very susceptible to changing economic conditions, the industry has become increasingly segmented, targeting specific customer niches. Chains have also become very popular.

RFS Hotel Investors, Inc.
889 Ridge Lane Blvd., Suite 220
Memphis, TN 38120
901-767-7005
Trades on the NYSE: symbol RFSI

Year	Change in Price per Share (%)	Yield (%)	Total Annual Return (%)
1996	28.5	8.8	37.3
1995	5.1	8.1	13.2
1994	-0.8	6.6	5.8

THE BOTTOM LINE

Direct ownership of income-producing property is not recommended for most people. If you're considering purchasing such a property, be sure to subject it to the bond test. Does the property perform at least as well as a high-yield bond?

The simpler and more reliable way for the average investor to take part in the growth of the real estate market is to invest in a real estate investment trust. Equity REITs are akin to owning stocks that specialize in real estate; mortgage REITs are more like owning mortgage-backed bonds. Though mortgage REITS are the safer of the two, even they can experience wide swings in returns. REIT investors should be prepared for highly uneven results.

As with all investments, past results are no indication of future returns.

Starwood Lodging Trust
2231 E. Camelback Rd., Suite 410
Phoenix, AZ 85016
602-852-3900
Trades on the NYSE: symbol HOT

Year	Change in Price per Share (%)	Yield (%)	Total Annual Return (%)
1996	85.3	6.9	92.2
1995	72.5	5.4	77.9
1994	9.5	0.0	9.7
1993	162.5	0.0	162.5
1992	14.3	0.0	14.3

Your Financial Plan

Now you know about all the major types of investments, and the vehicles you can use to make those investments. To be a successful long-term investor, though, you must have an overall financial plan. You don't want to make scattershot, individual investment decisions according to passing whims or market fluctuations.

Perhaps the best way to explain the importance of financial planning is by analogy. Suppose you are a cabdriver and have just picked up a fare. You ask your passenger where he wants to go and the passenger responds, "I'm not sure. The only thing I can tell you is that I want you to take me somewhere that is comfortable." To get a better idea as to what this person means, you ask some more questions: "What exactly do you mean by 'comfortable'—a place you can sleep, sit, have a drink, relax, see a movie? How far should I take you? Do you want to take a direct route or something more scenic? How much money can you spend on the cab fare and the place I might take you? How long do you want to stay at this place—should I wait for you? The response to all of these questions is "I don't know. I just want to be comfortable."

As ridiculous as this exchange sounds, this is *exactly* how most of us plan for our financial future. We all want to retire comfortably. We're just not sure what the best way to prepare for such retirement is.

What should you look for in an investment? Are the investments you have now the right ones for you? How can you reduce your overall investment risk? Your investment program should be carefully constructed to achieve your goals, without taking more risk than you are comfortable with or can afford. Whenever you make new investments you want to do so with the following questions in mind:

1. What financial goals do you want to achieve?

Your investments should always be driven by what you want to do with your money and when you want to do it. So the first step in building a portfolio is to identify your financial goals. You may want your investments to meet specific needs, such as buying a house or car, paying for college, or supplementing your retirement income. Or your goals may be more general—building up cash reserves or accumulating wealth. Either way, determining your objectives will help lead you to the most appropriate investments.

2. When do you hope to reach them?

Do you want to buy a house in five years or retire in twenty years? Will your eldest child enter college in nine years? Setting time horizons for your goals is critical. Different time horizons lead to different investment strategies. The sooner you need to spend the money you are investing, the more you need to focus on investments that preserve your principal and are easy to liquidate. Conversely, the longer you can leave your money invested, the less you need to worry about short-term price fluctuations and the more you can focus on earning the highest return over time.

3. How bold or cautious do you want to be?

Risk, return, and timing are all related. Generally, the riskier an investment, the higher its potential return over time and the more suitable it is for an investor with a longer-term horizon. But risk can be managed in different ways. One way is through what professionals call *asset allocation*—how you divide your money between stocks and bonds or other types of investment. The other way is by deciding how conservative, moderate, or aggressive you are in terms of risk and selecting investments appropriate to your level of tolerance. The next two sections look at these different approaches. In either case, you'll be diminishing risk by diversifying.

Stocks versus Bonds

One way to look at the puzzle is to focus on what percentage of your entire holdings (meaning retirement accounts, college education money, bank CDs, and real estate) should be in equity and what percentage should be in debt. As you've seen in the earlier chapters of this book, though there are thousands upon thousands of potential investments, all of which can be purchased directly or through mutual funds, annuities, and REITs, they all still fall into these two categories. Plus, as noted earlier, there are a number of hybrid investments—convertible securities, balanced funds, total return annuities, and hybrid REITs—that combine equity and debt in a single investment.

Stocks

Historically, equity has greatly outperformed debt. The price to be paid for such performance has usually been greater risk. As a whole, stocks are about twice as risky as bonds. However, the risk level of stocks drops quite dramatically if you own several stocks in different industries for at least a five-year period. If you can live with the daily ups and downs and keep a long-term perspective, the stock market becomes far less risky and less daunting. Furthermore, different types of stocks have different levels of risk. In general, a small company stock (a company that is worth $1 billion or less) is more risky than a mid-cap stock (market value of $2 to $5 billion) or a large company (or large cap) stock whose value is $6 to $20 billion or more.

Although these are the extremes, there are a couple of things you can learn from this. First, the potential loss on stocks can be quite severe. Second, historically, the worst year for even long-term bonds is only about a third of what it was for stocks. Third, medium-term bonds have about

How They Stack Up

Here is a look at the best and worst years for several different investment categories, and inflation overall, over the past half a century (1948–1997).

Category	Best Year	Return (%)	Worst Year	Return (%)
Small stocks	1967	84	1973	-31
S&P 500	1954	53	1974	-27
Long-term government bonds	1982	40	1967	-9
Medium-term government bonds	1982	29	1994	-5
U.S. Treasury bills	1981	15	1946	0
Inflation	1949	-2	1946	18

half the downside risk of their long-term counterparts, but three-fourths the upside potential.

Bonds

Like stocks, debt instruments have different characteristics and risk levels, but the boundaries can be defined more clearly. Maturity, quality and current yield, taken in order, determine virtually all of a bond's characteristics and risk.

• **The greater the maturity, the greater the risk.** A short-term bond fund (with an average maturity of five years or less) has less risk than an intermediate-term bond fund (one whose average maturity is six to ten years). In turn, the medium-term portfolio has less risk than a long-term bond fund (with an average maturity of eleven to thirty years).

• As you can guess, a **quality** bond portfolio has less risk than one whose average rating is below investment grade, meaning it has an overall rating of BB, B, CCC, CC, C, or D (for in default). But with professional management, the average quality of a bond fund's holdings often does not matter nearly as much as the average maturity. This is because the default rate of high-yield bonds normally becomes an issue only when we are in a severe recession.

• **The higher the yield, the lower the interest rate risk**. The income from the higher yield can offset some or all of any loss in a bond portfolio's value. Thus, if a bond fund's assets drop 4 percent during the year due to interest rate increases, interest

The Power of Compounding

Remember an important lesson from the first chapter: No matter where you invest, it's important to get started as soon as possible and invest as much as you can as regularly as you can. The following shows how dramatically regular monthly investments of $50, $200, or $500 can accumulate over time, assuming a 12 percent annual return.

Monthly Investment Amounts	5 years	10 years	20 years	25 years
$50	$3,810	$10,530	$43,230	$80,000
$200	$15,240	$42,120	$172,920	$319,990
$500	$38,100	$105,300	$432,300	$799,980

payments of 8 percent will easily wipe out that loss. If a bond drops 4 percent in value but pays 7 percent in interest, the total return is a positive 3 percent. When it comes to a bond portfolio's risk level, though, current yield is not nearly as important as maturity and quality.

Time Horizon

All other things being equal, the longer your horizon, the more your holdings should be in equities. This means that even a conservative investor should probably have most or all of his money in stocks (perhaps some of the less aggressive categories) if he can stay committed and live with the ups and downs for at least ten years. At the other extreme, an aggressive investor should most likely invest in stocks only if her time horizon is at least a few years.

Over the past half century, common stocks, as measured by the S&P 500, returned an average of 12 percent per year. Government and high-quality corporate bonds have returned less than half that.

The stock market certainly looks more appealing than bonds or money market instruments, but stocks have dropped more than 10 percent—and sometimes over 20 percent—in value over the course of a day, a month, a quarter, or a year, on more than one occasion. It would be extremely unlikely for a bond to have a total return of -10 percent for a similar period.

The table below shows how often stocks, as measured by the S&P 500, have outperformed long-term U.S. Government bonds over the past fifty years, assuming holding periods of different lengths, from 1948–1997.

Period of Time	Percent of Time Stocks Outperformed Bonds
All one-year holding periods	66 (50 different one-year periods)
All three-year holding periods	77 (48 different three-year periods)
All five-year holding periods	83 (46 different five-year periods)
All ten-year holding periods	93 (41 different ten-year periods)
All fifteen-year holding periods	100 (36 different fifteen-year periods)
All twenty-year holding periods	100 (31 different twenty-year periods)

If the past is any indication, and in fact I believe the advantage of stocks over bonds in the future will be even greater, even conservative investors should seriously consider a moderate or high allocation to stocks, particularly if their holding period is at least three years.

Risk Ranking

Deciding between stocks and bonds is one broad way of approaching asset allocation. With more detailed analysis, you can control risk even further by diversifying among different sectors of investing. When I work with my clients, I use the following table to help them determine an appropriate risk level. Unlike other risk tests, this table shows potential losses, the range of return one should expect, and how long it should take to make up the loss.

Risk Level	Annual Return (%)	Frequency of Loss	Range of Loss (%)	Recovery Time
1	5-6	No chance of loss *	—	—
2	8	1 in 12	0 to -3	6 months
3	10	1 in 10	0 to -6	9 months
4	12	1 in 8	0 to -7	10 months
5	14	1 in 7	0 to -9	14 months
6	16	1 in 6	0 to -12	16 months
7	17	1 in 5	0 to -16	22 months
8	18	1 in 4	0 to -20	25 months

Loss does not reflect the effects of inflation and income taxes.

This approach places all investments on a scale of 1 to 10, with 10 the highest level of risk. Up to a point, each additional increment of risk is a good trade-off between increased risk and increased return. However, once you go above a 7, the trade-off is no longer even—for every increase in risk level your return potential will not rise nearly as much. In other words, risk levels of 8 to 10 do not represent good or equitable *risk-adjusted* returns (you are not being properly compensated for the added amounts of risk).

• **The annual return** indicates on a compound basis the average yearly result over any given four- to six-year period.

• **The frequency of loss** indicates the odds that for any one year, your overall portfolio will show a loss (e.g., a 1 in 8 loss means that you will sustain a loss approximately once every eight years).

• **The range of loss** again is measured on an annual basis; any quarterly loss could be greater or less than what is shown.

• **The recovery time** notes the projected number of months it will take to earn back what is lost.

Once a client selects a comfortable risk level, I match it to a corresponding portfolio, samples of which are provided below, based primarily on a basket of mutual funds. I never recommend that anyone go above a 7, due to the relationship of risk and reward at such levels.

Extremely conservative (1)

10%	Utilities
10%	Balanced
10%	Convertibles
10%	High-yield bond
10%	World (international) bond
20%	Intermediate-term govern-ment (or municipal) bonds
30%	Cash (money market)

Conservative (2–3)

10%	Growth and income
10%	Global (world) stock
10%	Natural resources (or a mortgage REIT)
20%	Utilities
15%	Balanced
15%	Convertibles
20%	High-yield bond

Conservative to moderate (3–4)

10%	Growth (or an equity REIT)
10%	Growth and income
10%	Global (world) stock
10%	Natural resources
10%	Utilities
10%	Balanced
10%	Convertibles
20%	High-yield bond
10%	World (international) bond (or a mortgage REIT)

Moderate (5)

10%	Small company growth
15%	Growth (or an equity REIT)
15%	Growth and income
15%	Global (world) stock
10%	Natural resources
10%	Convertibles
15%	High-yield bond
10%	World (international) bond (or a mortgage REIT)

Fairly aggressive (6)

10%	Aggressive growth
20%	Small company growth
15%	Growth
15%	Growth and income (or an equity REIT)
25%	Foreign stock
15%	Natural resources

Aggressive (7–8)

20%	Aggressive growth
10%	Small company growth
10%	Growth
10%	Growth and income
20%	Foreign stock
15%	Emerging markets
15%	Natural resources

Build Your Own Portfolio

Of course you can and should be building your own portfolio with your own criteria in mind, whether you are working with a professional or doing it yourself. The following list provides another way of categorizing different types of investments in very general terms, this time based on their average annual returns:

Return: 3–5%

Assets to consider:

Bank CDs

Money market funds

U.S. Treasury bills (T-bills)

Tax-free money market funds

Passbook savings accounts

Return: 5–6%

Assets to consider:

Tax-free bonds maturing in ten years or more

U.S. Treasury notes (T-notes)

Fixed-rate annuities maturing in two to five years

Series EE Bonds

Series HH Bonds

Bank CDs maturing in five-plus years

Government bond funds

Personal residence

Tax-free bond funds

Return: 6–7%

Assets to consider:

U.S. Treasury bonds (T-bonds)

Corporate bonds maturing in three to seven years

Tax-free bonds maturing in fifteen-plus years

Fixed-rate annuities maturing in six-plus years

ARM (adjustable-rate mortgage) funds

Whole life insurance cash buildup

High-yield tax-free bond funds

FNMAs and GNMAs

Return: 8–9%

Assets to consider:

Preferred stocks

Foreign bonds

Global bond funds

High-yield corporate bonds

Mortgage REITs

Return: 10–11%
Assets to consider:
Convertible securities funds
Income funds
Balanced funds
Utility stock funds
Variable life insurance (equity subaccounts)
Metals (gold) funds
Hybrid REITs

Return: 12–13%
Assets to consider:
Utility stocks
Emerging markets bonds
Variable annuities (equity subaccounts)
Equity REITs

Return: 14–15%
Assets to consider:
Growth funds
Growth and income funds
Global equity funds
Individual blue-chip stocks

Return: 16–17%
Assets to consider:
Small cap growth funds
Aggressive growth funds
Individual OTC stocks
Emerging market stock funds
Foreign stocks and international stock funds

Diversify Your Assets

The examples below show how some typical investors used different mutual funds to diversify their assets in pursuit of their goals. By spreading your assets across a broad range of investments, you'll be sufficiently diversified to keep your risk at acceptable levels while you meet your goals. Now, based on what you know about your own goals, financial needs, and risk tolerance, you're ready to build your own portfolio.

Single person, 30
Total investments: $30,000
Risk profile: Conservative
Short-term goals: Cash reserves
Intermediate-term goals: Down payment on
    condominium
Long-term goals: Retirement

Long-term 60%

Short-term 20%

Intermediate-
term 20%

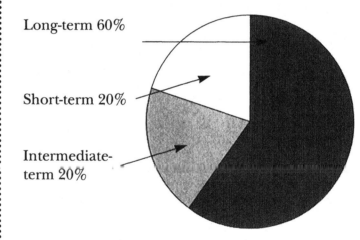

- Money market fund, 7%

- Adjustable-rate government securities fund, 13%

- Income fund, 20%

- Growth fund, 60%

John keeps about six months' living expenses in short-term investments—a money fund for stability of his principal and instant liquidity and a fund invested in adjustable-rate mortgage-backed securities for higher yield with minimal price volatility. He puts the remainder of his assets into an income fund to build capital for a condominium down payment in a few years, and a growth fund for his more distant retirement goal.

Married couple, both 45, with two children
Total investments: $200,000
Risk profile: Aggressive
Short-term goals: New car and cash reserves
Intermediate-term goals: College tuition
Long-term goals: Retirement

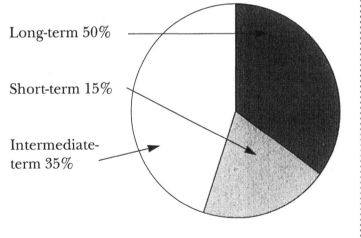

Long-term 50%

Short-term 15%

Intermediate-term 35%

Despite what has taken place in the stock market from the early-eighties, when the Dow bottomed out at 876 and then rose to over 9,000 by mid-1998, I have not heard or read about any individual investor who has actually experienced 16 or more percent returns over a ten- to fifteen-year period of time. There are literally dozens and dozens of equity funds that have enjoyed such returns, but very few investors actually stayed with such fund(s) for even most of the happy ride. Second-guessing management, constantly going into "hot" funds after existing funds or other investments were comparatively disappointing, being impatient overall has been the downfall of investors in general.

- Tax-exempt money market fund, 5%

- Tax-free intermediate-term bond fund, 10%

- Municipal bond fund, 15%

- Equity-income fund, 20%

- Growth fund, 15%

- Small cap growth fund, 20%

- Foreign stock fund, 15%

For short-term needs, this high-tax-bracket couple invests in short-term tax-free securities. For upcoming college bills, they choose investment-grade tax-free bonds and income-producing stocks. To maximize potential capital appreciation and inflation protection, their retirement money is invested in large- and small-company growth stocks as well as foreign blue chips.

Married couple, retired, both 65
Total investments: $40,000
Risk profile: Moderate
Short-term goals: Cash reserves and vacation money
Intermediate-term goals: Supplement pension and social security
Long-term goals: Maintain purchasing power

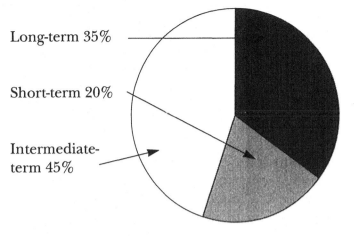

Long-term 35%

Short-term 20%

Intermediate-term 45%

- Money market fund, 10%

- Intermediate-term bond fund, 10%

- Government securities fund, 15%

- High-yield bond fund, 20%

- Balanced fund, 10%

- Growth and income fund, 15%

- Growth fund, 20%

For travel and emergencies, these retirees have a money market fund. Intermediate-term bonds, high-yield bonds, and longer-term government securities provide supplemental income and relative price stability. For inflation protection, continued capital growth and broad diversification, they choose a balanced fund of stocks and bonds, plus a growth and income fund and a growth fund.

Keeping Track

After you've started your investment program, the next logical question is "How often should I make changes in the portfolio?" Assuming that you've avoided ultra-conservative and wild investments, the answer is infrequently. Initially, I suggest the people review their holdings twice a year. Once you become comfortable or somewhat experienced with the ups and downs of the different marketplaces, an annual review is all that is necessary.

If you are in fundamentally good investments, you do not want to start second-guessing the stock, bond, or real estate markets. No one has successfully predicted what any investment market will do over any meaningful period of time. In fact, studies have shown that trying to time the market or using a timing service or newsletter (i.e., deciding when to be in and out of stocks, bonds, gold, etc.) actually decreases one's rate of return by 2 percent a year or more. The gap becomes even greater once taxes are factored in (every time an exchange takes place, a tax event is triggered—unless the money is inside an annuity or qualified retirement account).

What's Next

We have now gone full circle. In a relatively short period of time, you have learned about the differences among equity, debt, and hybrid instruments. The bias throughout the entire book has been toward equities: the different stock categories offered by mutual funds and variable annuities as well as REITs that are in the business of buying, managing, and selling properties.

Based on the track record over the past sixteen years (1983–1998) it would certainly be easy to make a case for equities, but we will only know in hindsight if such a period was a fluke or a sign of equal or better things to come. But the case for equities stretches back well over a hundred years. No one has ever *become* wealthy in debt instruments. Wealth creation takes place by ownership—owning a business, a piece of real estate, oil wells, or common stock (which represents partial ownership of a corporation).

Despite the convincing case for equities, do not let greed blind you; the disappointment, fear, and frustration that stockholders frequently experience is real, even though it is never reflected by some chart, table, or graph. Equities should be the cornerstone of your portfolio and your financial dreams *only* if you have the time and patience. Quick trades and constantly looking for the next "sure thing" turns investing into gambling.

Armed with the knowledge in this book, you are now ready to make informed decisions as to your and your family's future—a rich and rewarding one, *if you take the next step and act.* You may not like the stock, bond, or real estate market today, next month, or even next year. If this is the case, ease your dollars into your favorite marketplaces by investing a small portion of your portfolio each month or quarter. If this method of time diversification does not suit you, then resolve that if and when the market, be it stocks, bonds, or real estate, drops or rises by a certain specified amount, then you will invest. Set that goal and stick with it. Do not second-guess yourself or the market and sit on the sidelines for another period. If you do, you may never become a participant.

SMART MONEY

There are over a hundred timing services and newsletters that purport to know when to get into the market (a buy signal) and when to get out (a sell signal). The reality is that these sources are trying to sell you a false sense of security. If Alan Greenspan's money management firm (he was the principal of such a company just before he became head of the Federal Reserve) could not outperform the Dow or the S&P 500, what are the chances that some market timer can do better? Yet there will always be a handful of market timers who outperform the markets, at least on a pre-tax basis, since there are so many guessers. Unfortunately, like the performance of a REIT, variable annuity, or mutual fund, there is no relationship between past, present or future returns.

THE BOTTOM LINE

To invest soundly, you need to create an overall financial plan. Avoid scattershot investments that don't fit into your plan.

The keys to a good plan are identifying your goals, giving them a time frame, and deciding what level of risk makes you comfortable.

Generally speaking, most long-term investors should favor equities in their portfolios.

Always look for sound investments and investment professionals with a solid track record of good performance for a minimum of three to five years.

Finally, and most important of all, try to begin your investing program as soon as possible. Time and the power of compounding are an investor's greatest allies—the sooner you start, the better you will do.

Participating in a game is much more enjoyable than watching it. As we age, we reflect on the memories of things we actually did, not on the experiences of someone else. Making the decision to invest means that you are a participant. As an investor you will certainly experience the joys and sorrows of investing. But just like a winning athlete, with proper training, which this book provides, you can be a winner even though you won't be victorious every time.

Index

Books in the
Smart Guide™ Series

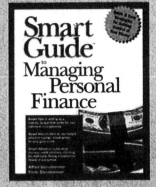

Smart Guide™ to
Getting Strong and Fit

Smart Guide™ to
Getting Thin and
Healthy

Smart Guide™ to
Making Wise
Investments

Smart Guide™ to
Managing Personal
Finance

Smart Guide™ to
Profiting from Mutual
Funds

Smart Guide™ to
Vitamins and Healing
Supplements

Available soon:

Smart Guide™ to
Boosting Your Energy

Smart Guide™ to
Healing Foods

Smart Guide™ to
Home Buying

Smart Guide™ to
Relieving Stress

Smart Guide™ to
Starting and Operating
a Small Business

Smart Guide™ to
Time Management